EXECUTIVE RETREATS FOR BUSY BUSINESS LEADERS

How to Achieve More by Working Less

David Achata

CONTENTS

FOREWORD

In 2018, I was serving as President and COO of a public semiconductor company when someone made a ten billion dollar offer to buy us. Just like that we were thrown into the high stakes whirlwind of a sales process and little did I know it would be my inciting incident for a storm that would come next. Here's a brief overview of my story:

Many years earlier I received a job offer with (what would become) my company shortly after graduating with my engineering degree from USF's College of Engineering. After having worked at that same organization for just over twenty years, I'd served in just about every function. When I first joined the company, we had around thirty-five million in annual revenue, but we had our sights on growing a lot more. It was always a high stress job with my role changing just about every two to three years as we grew. We completed multiple mergers and with each disruptive change, I received more responsibility. I learned to see disruption as an opportunity versus fearing it and to dictate the change rather than have it dictated to me.

BUILDING A SUCCESSFUL ORGANIZATION

I eventually landed the position of President and COO and our company's valuation surged during my tenure in that role with a multibillion-dollar market cap expansion. My job required that I grow accustomed to insane international travel schedules, impromptu presentations, and keynote engagements. Major market driven events required business plan pivots, and we kicked off multimillion-dollar investments that would take years to determine success or failure. Customer crises regularly required me to step in, and closing major deals became normal. I would owe my "success" to being a good problem solver, a chosen governing tenant of objectivity, understanding what motivated individuals, and focusing on building a team that had a culture which allowed us to excel. The latter two were not innate and required leadership development work which David Achata graciously helped me with.

My most treasured gift during my tenure was received after being named General Manager. I had been given responsibility for a business unit. My task was clear—to turn the business around. The business unit had gone through a few leaders already and as if in some twisted way of encouraging me, my boss told me not to get used to my office as it had a revolving door on it. During my first all hands meeting, it was clear the people were tired and discouraged, but after rebooting our business plan and creating a culture of accountability and an environment that made it safe to take risk and fail: the business thrived. The team executed and got us out of the rut, and I was promoted out of the position to embrace a new challenge. On my last day with that business unit, the group gave me a simple engraved wooden plaque that read *"To the General Manager that made a difference."* The difference they described wasn't about the metrics of success we were using, but the environment we created. The employees finally had the ingredients of job satisfaction: complexity, autonomy, a connection between reward and effort, and most importantly, purpose. I knew from my own experience that zero job satisfaction comes from simply being able to punch the clock.

While something in my wiring naturally drives me to solve problems, this gift was meaningful to me because I derive a great deal of satisfaction from being useful. There is nothing more satisfying for me than making a difference. Given what I did the majority of my waking hours, usefulness began to look like completing tasks and generating returns. Even on vacations I would try and sneak away to work without my family noticing—my wife would often ask if I was headed to do work and remind me that I needed time to decompress. Robin William's character in the movie, "RV", pretends to have bowel trouble so he can type out a presentation on his phone while sitting on the toilet all without his family noticing—*I was that guy!*

At the time of the offer to buy the company, our culture felt a bit like family. Over the years, we worked hard to achieve our stated goals. I owe our success to a sense of personal accountability each of us had. We were pretty hard on ourselves because we didn't want to let each other down. It was especially difficult and hurtful when the sale process started to divide us.

HOW IT ALL ENDED

In every acquisition there is an attempt to make one plus one equal three and that process is called synergy capture: it's a fancy way of saying that you're eliminating redundant positions. If you place a large pile of money in the middle of a team and they have the understanding that their positions will soon be eliminated, the natural question that creeps up within each person is ... how much of that pile do I get? Some diverted energy to ensuring that transaction happened at any cost hoping for a windfall exit and still others focused on it not being the end. We were a public company and the lawyers would periodically remind everyone of what Fiduciary Duty and Breech of Loyalty meant, but people's emotions tend to take over in that environment. You don't often see divided management teams during a transaction, but during one of the most stressful times of our company's history, the "family" had the added pressure of being split apart! Volatile meetings, side conversations, disinvites to major decision discussions were par for the course, we resembled a season of Survivor. We exhibited an ugly side of business at times; in a manner that I found abhorrent. It was nothing like who we were before.

It was especially lonely for me during this time. I had to keep the company operating and meeting its performance targets while putting on a brave face for the employees all the while knowing I would soon be out of a job. Thankfully a select few of us were able to remain steadfast and "do right" by the organization; we secured retention packages for the employees which would cushion the blow felt with the ensuing terminations and ensure continuation of operations. Despite our best efforts, there was still a lot of bitterness that would inevitably be directed at me and the rest of management—we had created something special and most didn't want it to end, but fiduciary responsibility meant we were legally obligated to drive the best return for shareholders and finish the deal.

ACTIVITY ADDICTION

At the close, I was let go as anticipated. It was a bittersweet moment for me. I had presided over what most would classify as a success. While it should have been a moment to catch my breath, for some reason, the inability to continue the pace I'd been on for the last twenty years made me extremely anxious. I started filling my time with tasks and other distractions because of a strange notion that I might get lazy if I stopped running, but the reality was that I wasn't comfortable sitting still. I was feeling useless as I was no longer driving a business. I talked a lot about taking a moment to contemplate what I was going to do next knowing that was the right thing to do, but I didn't do it. I jumped in to help a small startup for zero compensation which ended up being as stressful as what I'd just come from, if not more. I had gotten used to the pace I'd been running at and (in fact) found a sick comfort in it. As David lays out for busy business leaders: I needed to go away but wouldn't allow myself.

In a short period of time after the close, my dog died, my sister died, my dad died, and my house burned down in a California wildfire. My wife would ask me how I was feeling periodically, and my response was always "I'm fine," and I thought I was! She would remind me that FINE stood for Feelings Inside Never Expressed—she was right. I continued coping with the stress of life I was under with constant distraction until my wife pressed in and said she was worried about me. She noticed I was falling asleep during the day and that was something I had never done. She feared something was wrong with my health and asked me to get a complete workup. She was right again!

THE IMPACTS ON MY BODY

After a complete battery of tests, this Doctor who I had never met walked in and said, "well I can tell you just went through an extremely stressful time in your life." *What?!? How can bloodwork and a hormone panel tell that?* I wondered. Turns out I was in adrenal fatigue. She told me I had the energy of an 85-year-old which didn't sit well with a competitive almost 50-year-old man. All my healthy blood indicators had plummeted.

If the body is a biological machine, life (with a little help from me) had pushed mine way beyond its redline and something had to give. The good news was that, with stopping and focusing on rebuilding my body and mind, I could recover.

I always knew that stress could have a profound effect on my health and I've always attempted to eat healthy and exercise as a means of dealing with it and then keep pressing on. It certainly helped me cope in the past, but I had tested and greatly exceeded my body's limits. I failed to take the time to truly process both the disruptive career changes and the profound losses of my family members. Instead, I was coping by piling on incessant distraction, which is not coping, it's avoidance. The pressure cooker was debilitating. I had always reminded myself that "no one on his deathbed ever said, 'I wish I had spent more time on my business,'" but I was focused on busyness anyway. It was time to go away and put in the work necessary to get my bearings.

WHAT IT LOOKED LIKE FOR ME TO GO AWAY

I finally did take that break. I started with the basics and focused on diet and exercise leveraging the work ethic and diligence I had always employed. I also spent a lot of time alone with my thoughts, chopping wood of all things. When I get into nature, without distraction, time seems to slow, and I have time to process what I'm feeling. I made time for introspection. In the stillness,

I started asking myself if the job wasn't my identity, who was I? Instead of busyness, I started focusing on breakfast dates with my kids, dates with my wife, and silly time with the grandkids—all with my phone turned off. I took trips to go see my mom just to spend uninterrupted time talking and reminiscing. I started mentoring other young men which is an amazing exercise; you get to go through all the things you've learned on your journey and they sometimes ask questions you've never thought of. Fundamentally my focus shifted during this time. I learned that I could be useful to people by pouring into relationships as well as accomplishing business outcomes.

With renewed focus, I joined a small tech company as CEO once again hoping to make a difference by focusing on building a team culture that would allow us to excel. Though I hold things a little more loosely than I did before, I'm still driven. When things aren't done to our best capability it drives me insane, but now I try to focus on effecting the change I'm able to. One thing is for certain, without going away, I likely would have been a liability to my new team rather than an asset.

CONCLUSION

The principles David lays out in his book emphasize an often-overlooked part of the process of leadership. Leaders must take the time necessary to plot their organization's development course which is a lot more than just a vision and mission statement. The military has an expression—slow is smooth and smooth is fast. Applied to business leadership this means that leaders must slow down to gain the situational awareness necessary to implement the changes for smooth operations; doing so speeds up the achievement of desired outcomes. The exhaustion of life forced me to slow down to get healthy. Yet burnout isn't inevitable. You can implement the wisdom of slowing down long before trouble strikes, so read the coming pages with focus.

Take care of yourself. All great leaders exhibit one profound skill—self-awareness. Tending to your development will be the secret to unlocking the best in you, and those around you, thereby accelerating the success of your important work in this world.

Paul Pickle
President/CEO, Lantronix
Irvine, California

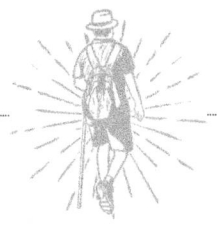

"Without great solitude, no serious work is possible."

—Pablo Picasso

PREFACE

I vaguely remember when I lost my mind. It was a cold night in the winter of 2015, and I couldn't sleep. My mother had died a few days before, and I was getting readjusted to the normal world after helping care for her in the final months of her life. Tossing and turning, I was buried in a fog of memories, the kind that come with the loss of a parent, but this was so much more, too.

In the years previous, I'd moved my family multiple times, from Orlando to Portland, to Seattle, and to Southern California. I'd left a career as a pastor and started a small consulting company. Things were up and down, but after about six years, we finally started to feel stable.

I'd settled into (what I thought was) a healthy rhythm. One of my clients was a worldwide microchip company that kept me busy helping merge teams after acquisitions. I traveled regularly for work with my other clients too. In addition to this, I was helping to start a new church in the city where we lived. My plate was full, but I was having fun. I liked being busy and had something planned for every hour of the day. But during my "healthy rhythm," I had a few "minor" problems I'd been managing for years.

Our finances were unpredictable. One month there was plenty of money; others, not so much. Years of living this way had worn me down. At home, it took considerable work to maintain the household, as my wife suffered from chronic illness and migraines. During that time, we also discovered my son had a minor case of Cerebral Palsy. This required extra visits to doctors and physical therapists. *Not a big deal*, I thought. *This is just my own version of life, and I'm going to hit it with everything I've got.*

As if the clients, traveling, helping start a new church, or all the family issues weren't enough, when my mother's cancer made a resurgence and there was no one to care for her, I did what I always did: I stepped in and took over. I didn't realize it then, but I had a big problem. I was overly responsible. My eye to fix broken things was getting the better of me. At the time, it looked and felt impressive. But, as you'll see in a moment, living this way would eventually cause me to lose my ability to work effectively (or accomplish anything).

By concerning myself with others and their chaos, I was unable to face the problems in my own life. I was enmeshed, co-dependent, and my inner life couldn't bear the emotional weight of the responsibility I was surrounded by.[1] So what did I do? I suppressed my feelings and worked harder for everyone because I dreaded

---

1   Through the ACA program (Adult Children of Alcoholics and Dysfunctional Families®), I've learned that children of dysfunctional families often bear the trait of over-responsibility. The term "Adult Child" refers to doing certain work in the world with the emotional life of a child. It doesn't mean one can't do great work. It just means one's internal life may not be as mature as necessary. See the ACA Fellowship Text (The Big Red Book), 2006. p.14

failure and the disapproval (or potential collapse) of my personal and work relationships. Rather than asking for help, I drowned my life in a flood of duties and neglected myself, thinking everyone needed me.[2] But what did *I* need? What was good for *me*? I wasn't ready to ask those questions yet.

For nearly six months, my life became a mix of lonely flights between Tennessee (where my mother lived) and California, sleepless nights, oncology visits, corporate clients, church work, and tears.

When my mother passed on, I was left to deal with my grief and all the "minor" problems I'd not fully attended to in the years previous. I'd been living for so long in urgent mode, and I'd not attended to the important. I'd let my health slide, my relationship with my wife was distant, and I'd not grieved all the losses from years of nomadic living. We'd taken a lot of risks, and we were damaged. I learned the hard way during that time that a healthy person can endure a lot of deficiency. But an unhealthy person? Without a relative amount of health in the basic areas of life (financial, personal health, important relationships, and purpose[3]), an unhealthy person will become decimated with a major loss. It was time for me to pay the price of a lifetime of helping others succeed and not properly caring for

---

2 Ibid., p. 94
3 For more information on the components of well-being, see https://www.gallup.com/workplace/237020/five-essential-elements.aspx

myself. I (like you) am a biochemical machine and run best when I fuel myself correctly. I'd not done that for a long time, and I finally cracked.

On that wintry, sleepless night, I dreamed a strange dream. In it, I believed my mother was still alive and needed care. In my sleep-deprived state, I woke and startled, thinking her dead body was beside me. I leaned over to touch it and it came to life! The face morphed, twisted, and changed. Like a strange LSD trip, before my eyes, the shape turned into my wife's. "What are you doing?" she whispered. I don't remember my reply. I shook the hallucination and muttered something, trying to go back to bed.

Things got worse.

I couldn't find the dishes in my own cabinets. I developed chronic pain in my stomach and hands. I lost the ability to focus, began getting lost in my own neighborhood and on the highway. For a short time, I even had to stop driving. My lack of focus became dangerous. Something had to change.

Life will bring terrible storms. If you haven't cared for yourself along the way, you *will* go down. I went down—hard. My anxiety spiraled out of control, and I ended up in a doctor's office with EKG wires taped to my chest. "I'm afraid I'm headed for a heart attack," I told her. After reading the report, she said, "You're perfectly healthy. Will you tell me what kind of stress you've been under?"

After unpacking the previous years of my life, she responded in empathetic and directive tones, "You could benefit from getting into a quieter environment." I discussed her advice with my wife, Amy, and we decided to listen. A few months later, we left California.

We moved to Tennessee to grieve, rest, and refocus. What we thought would be one year turned into many, and we're still here. Tennessee has been the quiet space we needed to get steady again, and I'm grateful for it. Losing my focus was hard, losing my former self (the one that took on too much), even harder. One reason it's so difficult to change is that we all adopt coping skills that get us to a certain point in life. But one day, when those coping skills stop working, it can still feel impossible to let them go. My body forced me to learn better mechanisms to operate by, and it's a journey I'm still on.

MY REAL PROBLEM

Not everyone has an extreme story of burnout like mine. But I've worked with enough leaders to know that, sadly, it's common. After thinking on it for a few years now, I see how my problems weren't primarily external. Instead, I see how the outside world reflected what was going on in my internal world. *I* needed attention, which manifested in my tending to all the disordered things around me. Could I just drop it all, take a breath, and get away? Not a chance. There were too many things only I could fix (I thought). Others would have called me "driven," but do you know what I really was? I was blind to my brokenness.

I've heard it said that if you don't rest, sickness will become your rest, and that's what happened to me. Though my mind felt lost, my body knew what to do. Listening to it, I began to retreat intuitively. I realized I had to go away. It started first by taking a few days away to hike in the desert during winter. Then a few weeks later, I did it again, taking a few days at a local state park. I started incorporating times away with my family, too (though it was initially my wife's idea). I came home one day from a short walk, and she said, "Get in the car. We're going on a camping trip for a few days. Everything's packed." I'm grateful for her. She knew I'd lost the ability to plan, so she helped me (more on this later).

Up to that point in my life, I'd not seen much of an example of someone going away to be more intentional with their lives. The only examples I'd seen were men who worked themselves to death. My burnout taught me to form a healthier environment for myself. Now, I affectionately call it "an ecosystem of wisdom." This ecosystem is made up of significant people and important containers of time spent together. In different seasons, I work with a spiritual director, various counselors, coaches, and mentors. I also take intentional times away to plan and rest. But above all, I now see my work as part of this ecosystem. These relationships and habits aren't what I do in my free time; they are part of my rhythm of healthy work. I still get off track sometimes, but when I feel a check in my gut, or a sharpness in my chest, I don't ignore it anymore.

You may be overlooking the check in your gut right now. Or maybe you've received feedback that you're not proud of. I want to encourage you, listen to your body or the feedback you're receiving. I didn't want to work less and focus on myself either because I felt that too much depended on me. Today, however, I've learned how to achieve a better outcome.

EXPAND YOUR DEFINITION OF WORK

Studies have shown that the average manager or executive works 51 or more hours[4] a week, while the average American works 38.7.[5] What if you took those extra eleven hours (or more) a week and applied them toward taking care of yourself? At your level, you can't sustain the non-stop action of a leadership role without time away. At some point, you've got to shift your value away from what you do to who you are.

What if you could achieve more by working less? To put it another way, what if your work was about

_____

4   https://www.bizjournals.com/kansascity/stories/2009/07/27/daily29.html
5   https://www.thebalancemoney.com/what-is-the-average-hours-per-week-worked-in-the-us-2060631

more than the hours you put in at the office? What if your job included time to take care of yourself so you could focus on *all* the places that matter? Soon, we'll unpack what this can look like. But for now, I want to say this: *You're not a human-doing. You're a human-being.*

For me, extreme measures were needed to move from doing to being. For you, maybe it simply needs to start with a half-day per month (during your work week). I don't know what you need, but your body probably knows. Have you slowed down to listen to it?

When we ignore our bodies too long, we lose the ability to detect true danger and harm. On the other hand, we also get numb so we don't know what is really safe and nourishing. This brings us to the place where we have to "rely on external regulation—from medication, drugs like alcohol, constant reassurance, or compulsive compliance with the wishes of others."[6] The life of a leader is ripe with these threats. But you can put in a safeguard.

You can go away.

EXECUTIVE RETREATS

Don't worry; you don't have to disappear from your life completely, though you may wish this sometimes. By "go away," I mean create the habit of regular strategic

---

6   Van Der Kolk, Dr. Bessel. *The Body Keeps the Score: Brain, Mind, and Body in the Healing of Trauma.* New York, Penguin Books, 2014. p. 99

spaces for yourself, your development, your team, and your family. In other words, executive retreats (think: focus times for anyone with a senior level of responsibility). The great part about these times away is that *you* choose what's most important and focus there. What would that mean for you?

Take a moment now. Close your eyes, breathe deep. What comes to mind as essential to pay attention to? Start with yourself. What's most important? Then work your way outward to your other levels of responsibility. Pause.

Now, write down what's come to your mind below.

Chances are, what you just wrote has something to do with your health, your focus, or the health of those you lead (including your family). This book is an invitation for you to go away to pay attention to that. You deserve it. You need it. Don't simply take the words "go away" to mean "check out of your work, your family, and your life."

Retreating isn't giving up, and it's not weak. Retreating is actually a very effective tool in your toolbelt that could help you win in many of the areas you're struggling. And I can say from experience, it's one of the tools used least by overly responsible leaders. You don't have to mirror the chaos around you. Instead, you can choose to do something counter-intuitive. In the craziness of life and work, why not do something that deescalates the busy pace of normal life? Even in battle, retreats have helped win wars.

RETREATS WIN WARS

I live in east Tennessee, not far from the north Georgia border. Historic signs dot the backroads that mark places of infamous battles and marches from the Civil War. Just minutes from my house is the Chickamauga Battlefield, where some of the bloodiest days of the war unfolded. Here's the story of that battle, and how a retreat helped the Union win the Civil War.

From September 18–20, 1863, Confederate and Union troops met at Chickamauga to fight for the region leading toward Chattanooga. Chattanooga was one of the most coveted cities in the South, because it was a central point where both railroad and river passed through. Whoever possessed Chattanooga would have a valuable asset by which to send much-needed resources to their army.

At the battle of Chickamauga, the Confederacy outnumbered the Federals, 65,000 to 60,000. Casualties numbered 16,170 Confederate and 18,454 Federal— a total of 34,624 lives impacted. It was the second most costly battle of the Civil War, ranking only behind the battle of Gettysburg. It was considered a victory for the Confederate States of America.[7]

The Union army retreated. Who knows what might have happened if the Confederate troops had pursued the retreating and fragmented Union army? But they did not. This is where the story takes a surprising turn. Rather than chasing down their defeated foe, the Confederates opted to bolster their positions on the mountain tops surrounding Chattanooga, planning to later lay siege to the city.

Two months passed. What would happen?

The Union Army rested, reconvened, and made a new plan. On November 24th, 1863, they re-emerged and attacked the high places where the Confederates

---

7 https://www.battlefields.org/learn/articles/10-facts-battle-chickamauga

camped, literally driving the rebels off the mountain tops. On Lookout Mountain, an icon of Chattanooga, the Confederates overestimated their advantage while taking aim at Union troops. Aiming their cannons down the steep decline, the Confederate cannon balls rolled harmlessly out of their cannons.[8] Unable to fire upon the enemy, the Confederates had to abandon their positions.

When my clients join me in Tennessee for retreats, I often take them to walk the hallowed grounds of Chickamauga Battlefield and tell them the story of how this tactical victory actually turned into a strategic defeat. Then, I'll drive them a few minutes away up to Point Park on Lookout Mountain. Walking the park, I'll tell them the story of The Battle Above the Clouds where the Confederates overestimated their advantage.

"Can you imagine going to fire on your enemy, only to discover your cannon balls rolling out?" I'll ask. Often, great pride accompanies success, but it can sometimes lead to a great fall.[9] "There's a place for strategic retreat," I say to my clients. "Don't get so lost in your smaller battles that you lose sight of your strategic goals."

Indeed, you can win a battle, but lose a war. That's what happened to the Confederacy. Though the

---

8   https://en.wikipedia.org/wiki/Battle_of_Lookout_Mountain

9   For more on this topic, see Jim Collins book *How the Mighty Fall: And Why Some Companies Never Give in*. In his model, the first stage that leads to an organization's demise is "Hubris born of success."

Union Army retreated after losing Chickamauga, they used their retreat strategically. The result? They won Chattanooga and eventually the Civil War.

THE BENEFITS OF RETREAT

We too can easily get lost in the day to day and find ourselves feeling alone and disoriented. But what if we practiced the art of retreat? Doing so could be the very thing you need to remember you are not alone, and you are more equipped than you think. Without retreat, it's easy to get lost in the non-stop gears of the corporate machinery.

Just yesterday, I met with a steady and confident CEO of a large company here in Chattanooga. She said, "At this level, I'm grasping to find out how I'm doing. When I was in a Vice President role, I had all kinds of feedback. But no one is giving me that feedback anymore. I have to go find it." She is wise. She knew she had to make time away to hear voices of wisdom and direction. In her case, she made time to discuss her situation with the CEO of a partner organization. This enabled her to come back focused and ready to lead. Retreats provide other benefits as well.

It's your internal life that fuels your outer work. So it's vital that you make times to rest and work on your character and intellect. How can you give to others if your reserves are depleted? How can you give to your closest teammates and family if you're tapped out? In the event of a rapid descent, flight attendants say, "Put your own oxygen mask on before attempting to help others." It's the same for you.

In addition to your health and the health of your family, you need time to allow your sights to be lifted to the higher purpose for which you're leading. Your work serves a purpose, so only you can set certain strategic plans. Do you want to set an example of someone whose life is dictated by daily tasks and interruptions? Sure, that's part of the work, but that's not your job. Your job is to remind people of the reason they are doing what they are doing. You're not just a CEO, CFO, or CMO; you're really a "CPO": Chief Purpose Officer.

Employee satisfaction comes from being challenged, having a part, and understanding the higher cause of their work.[10] The next generation is even more altruistic than the last, so you've got to get this right. Going away systematically will help retune your focus to the purpose aspect of your work.

THE 4 DISCIPLINES OF RETREAT

Being "on" all the time will kill you. It will kill your team and (eventually) your family. I want to save you from that and help you see how four disciplines (if you'll

---

10   See Daniel Pink's research in, *Drive: The Surprising Truth About What Motivates Us.*

integrate them) can make you happier, healthier, and more effective.

1. Go away alone.

2. Go away with a guide.

3. Go away with your team.

4. Go away with your family.

Here's why these disciplines are so important: They will multiply who you are within your organization. So briefly, here's why these four disciplines matter.

Discipline 1: Go Away Alone

Modeling what it looks like to go away alone to embody your values and have a life outside of work will help you be more engaged. It will also show your people that retreating and resting is normal, and what it can look like. The outcome: They'll be more engaged, too.

Discipline 2: Go Away with a Guide

Going away with a guide helps you stay aligned with your values and discern how your unique calling expresses itself within your organization. Outcome: A clear vision. This saves you from having to fight the many competing visions people will bring in the absence of a clear and compelling one.

Discipline 3: Go Away with Your Team

Taking strategic times away with your team will not only help you develop trust, and have some fun, but it will provide you an opportunity to think strategically in a world where tactics always seem to shout louder. Outcome: you'll create healthy relationships and intentional plans. This will help your team produce better organizational results vs. getting hung up in negative interpersonal dynamics that can happen in the absence of clear alignment.

Discipline 4: Go Away with Your Family

Going away with your family is about learning to embrace your own version of normal life. It's not about epic vacations, but great relationships with those closest to you. "Culture" is code for "relationships." Therefore, your organizational culture, the system of relationships in your workplace, can mimic the pace you set. Outcome: By modelling how to embrace your spouse and children, your people will see how they can do it too. The best result? You'll be a much happier person.

This is why you've got to go away. Invest in yourself, your team, and in your family. It will pay off personally and in your organization. I promise. So, as we begin, I want to pause with you to understand the words *executive*, and then, the word *retreat*.

RE-THINK EXECUTIVE, RE-THINK RETREAT

The word *executive* shares the same root as *execution*, which means "the carrying out of plans, order, or a course of action." How powerful you are! If you're in charge of anything (especially a business), then you're an executive. Stop to consider that you have the power to bring attention to places of need. Your role and title are rooted in the Latin, "exequi," a word which simply means; to accomplish. You're in an important seat; are you using it for its intended purpose?

Retreat comes from two Latin words; "Re" + "trahere." These words together mean "to draw back" to a "tract," or "an original place." Successful leaders find ways to go away regularly to remember who they are and where they're going. They leave their workplaces and go to an actual spot to think, recharge, and rest. Here's why— the higher you go in an organization, the heavier the emotional weight. Take care of yourself. No one else will.

My hope for you is that reading this book will inspire you to carry out plans to draw back to a "tract," or a literal place. It will change everything for you, your team at work, and your family. Burnout forced me to retreat to find my health again. Now, I retreat so I *stay* healthy.

Near the beginning of each year, I go away to look at the work that needs to be done and make purposeful plans. But the "work" I plan is about more than money-making. I take a careful look at my emotional health, my family, and those I work with. My thinking includes strategic planning to "draw back" to literal places for purposes of investing in each of these important areas of my life and to decide how I'm going to carry out those plans.

WHO THIS BOOK IS FOR

I wrote this book for overly responsible leaders. You're probably doing a great job leading your organization, but you may be tired, for any number of reasons, or looking for a way to grow in your influence. What would it mean for you to delegate some of what you're doing so you can take time to take care of yourself and focus? Stop to consider the positive impacts this could have, not only on your organization, but on you.

Clients come away on retreat with me for three reasons:

1. They are facing a key season of work and need to get centered to endure and plan for the important time ahead.

2. They are doing a great job at work, but their personal lives are holding them back in some way.

3. They've just gone through a difficult season of sorts and need to get recharged and focused for however they want to move forward.

In each case, these types of clients really need the same thing. Time away, alignment with their values and calling, and intentional planning. Whichever description you most identify with, the pathway is the same.

In my work coaching executives, I've met plenty of admirable men and women who have mastered the art of going away. Much of what you're about to read comes from the lessons gleaned while coaching them. If you're one of the disciplined ones, great! Please connect with me and share your secrets. I hope this book will also aid you on your continued journey toward greater impact.

Yet, for every healthy leader, I've met at least ten more who are struggling. Hidden behind a good outfit and a nice office, danger often lurks in the background. I've seen marriages on the rocks, kids in treatment programs, team members in silos, and organizations that resemble the wild west. If you relate with any part of that last sentence, this book is especially for you. The idea for this book came out of my own unhealth. For a long time, I believed I needed to be everything to everyone (at all times), and it led to my own mental and physical breakdown. Drastic measures had to be put in place, and I'm a different man today because of it. I'll tell you more of my story along the way.

To illustrate the importance of leadership health, I want to introduce you to a man I admire. He's one of the most remarkable and driven people I've met. But when I first made his acquaintance, though he had many great qualities, he had one quality that was derailing everything: he wouldn't go away. Here's an introduction to his story.

A SUCCESS STORY

Many years ago, I met Warren Johns (not his real name) when he and his wife Kelly moved to Orlando to take a job at a local hospital. Warren excelled at nearly everything he touched, but he also worked around the clock. Kelly asked him to be at home more, and Warren tried. But no matter his efforts, he still read emails until late. After a few years of high performance, Warren was promoted to an executive position in another state with the same health system. Warren and Kelly hoped the move would create a reset for their family. And it did for a little while.

About a year later, Warren reached out to me for help. His work life had spiraled out of control. Upon entering his new job, he reorganized his marketing team and significantly disrupted the status quo. Yet, despite his success, life came crashing down when his wife Kelly was put on bedrest due to a highly complicated preg-nancy, risking both the life of his wife and developing daughter. He couldn't figure out how to do what needed to be done at work *and* care for her. Kelly's emergency dictated change.

Through regular coaching conversations, and a two-day retreat, Warren realized his wife's health was forcing him to change. He had to find a way to leave work in order to care for her. So he created a plan to be more present with her, delegated at work, and started tending to his wife's needs and his own.

Life's surprises can actually be invitations to retreat. In Warren's case, his wife's pregnancy is what dictated the change. Sometimes, though, the surprises may not be dictated by one's home life. Sometimes the surprise could be an issue at work, missed financial targets, or even just plain exhaustion. Whatever the case, the answer is usually found in taking time to look inward, finding clarity, and forging a new path ahead. This is what Warren did, and his change was noticeable.

Warren began leaving the office on time. He poured his time into his wife's care and even decorated her hospital room as a visual masterpiece of their 14 years of marriage. He brought in a slate waterfall, a quilted bed spread, and over 500 photos that covered the walls in every direction Kelly looked. People began to marvel at what had happened.

Warren began to lead differently, too. He empowered his team to take ownership of things he'd been doing, which ended up multiplying his impact. His team noticed the change in his behavior and learned to trust him more. Warren's hands were no longer in the details, and he began leading at a higher level. Best of all, his wife began to believe she was valued, and Warren's life took a new direction. At the end of this book, I'll tell you more of his story.

LEADERSHIP IS A GIFT

This kind of thing doesn't happen by working longer hours. It happens when you start to go away. In Warren's case, he went away to focus on his wife. The thing is, others saw it and began to believe they could do it, too. Behavior trickles down.

You don't have to wait for your personal or work life to fall apart. You can go away now. Throughout this book, I'll share stories of others who have done this too. Maybe you've become a micromanager (which will limit your success) or are leading in ways you're not happy with. Perhaps your focus is scattered. Whatever's happening at work that's starting to "not work anymore," don't be foolish. Stop and notice the signs. You can do something about it.

People grant authority to those they see "authoring" their own lives. This is why these words share the same root. If you follow a script for what you think you should be doing, you'll be surrounded by others who do the same. What they'll never tell you though is that, as the leader, you're writing the script that others will follow. That script is your life.

Are you ready to author your own leadership and see the changes unfold? I'm here to help. I wrote this for you out of the script of my life.

David Achata
Founder, The Achata Coaching & Leadership Group

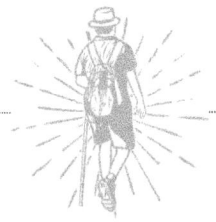

"Strategy without tactics is the slowest route to victory. Tactics without strategy is the noise before defeat."

—Sun Tzu

INTRODUCTION:
JOIN ME ON RETREAT

"Thousands of tired, nerve-shaken, over-civilized people are beginning to find out that going to the mountains is going home; that wildness is a necessity; and that mountain parks and reservations are useful not only as fountains of timber and irrigating rivers, but as fountains of life."

–John Muir, *Our National Parks*, 1901

It was a mild winter day on the coast of Northern New England. I'd flown there to meet Harry (not his real name) who was about to become CEO of a large pharmaceutical company. I'd been working with Harry for a year but had never met him in person. Months earlier, I suggested we plan a two-day retreat before he took the new role. We both liked mountain biking, so we planned a trip around that.

"David?" Harry asked, as I exited the airport carrying my backpack full of mountain biking gear. "It's me!" I responded. "It's great to meet you in person finally."

During our previous coaching sessions by phone, I'd learned a lot about Harry. He was an accountant by trade but had worked his way up in his organization. He had a family, too: a wife and two small children. Prior to working with Harry, I'd worked with his boss, who was the CEO of Harry's organization.

"Would you consider coaching the man I think will be my successor?" the CEO asked.

"If we're a good match, I'd be happy to," I said. One thing led to another, and here we were. Just a week away from Harry taking the CEO role I'd talked about with his predecessor many months before.

Walking toward the vehicle outside the airport, I took note of Harry's stature. He wasn't as tall as I imagined, but in person, his eyes were far more intense. Harry didn't drive a fancy car, but a full-size pickup that was a few years old. "You like my truck?" Harry asked as he saw me eyeing it. "I drive it on purpose. I don't want people in my company to be distracted by what I drive. People are suspicious enough these days about executives." I was quietly impressed. Harry seemed to behave in a very calculated way, and I wondered what else we'd discuss on the ride to the venue where we'd be staying.

I've worked with many leaders like Harry. At first meeting, they present confident and focused. But I've learned to wait for what they're secretly thinking about. That's the real reason I'm there. Standing on the curb outside Harry's truck, I thought about these things and changed the subject.

"I'm pretty hungry," I said, "where can we get something to eat?"

After pulling over for a burrito, we hit the road again and passed the time by talking about everything from bikes to our plans for life. We talked about our wives, our kids, and shifted the conversation to the needs of his organization. Before we knew it, the long drive was over. Unpacking and getting more comfortable, we met up a few hours later for dinner and a glass of wine.

"Here's the real reason I wanted to do this trip," Harry said. "Right now, I'm having more money thrown at me than I've ever seen in my life. I want to make sure I'm staying focused and not selling my soul."

After a pause to gather my thoughts, I asked, "What does it mean to *sell your soul*?"

"It would mean giving my whole life to this job," Harry said. "My phone is already ringing non-stop and, though I have people to help me, I need to monitor myself internally to make sure I'm healthy and paying attention to the right things."

"What are the right things?" I inquired.

"I think the right things have to do with my own health, my family, and to make sure I'm staying true to the vision I have for the organization, instead of just trying to climb the ladder and build job security," he said. A good start, but I wanted to dig even deeper.

"What do you mean when you say, 'job security?'" I asked.

"I want to set the expectation with my team that none of us are here to build a career. I don't want people like that on my team. I want people here who are here to serve our constituents," Harry said. Again, I was impressed and wondered what else was going on inside this interesting person.

There isn't time to share all the important conversations we had on this trip. What I will tell you is that these conversations have continued now over many years. But at that first retreat, Harry got honest about how he needed help disciplining himself to stay focused in his life and in his organization.

Coaching leaders for a long time now, I've learned that if you coach the person, problem solving comes a lot easier. Do it the other way around, and it's a recipe for a short relationship. The occasion of this retreat was to plan Harry's first ninety days as CEO, but what Harry really needed was to look deeper. Every retreat looks different, but they bear commonalities. Here's what we did for Harry.

Our first day together, we looked at Harry's personality and life priorities, then we took off for a mountain bike ride while talking about the morning's takeaways along the way. Our second day, we took the morning to look at Harry's first ninety days as CEO and made a plan for what he wanted to accomplish. Then we left for more outdoor activity along the coast. Simple, right?

On the surface, it must have looked like to two guys just having fun in the great outdoors. But underneath, it was more profound. In the act of Harry going away on a retreat, as Muir would say, he was really "going home." What I think Muir meant was that when we get away from the non-stop rush of activity, we find space to remember who we are, our values and main concerns.

Harry worked hard to make time for this. Though he had to take an urgent call once or twice, our time was mostly uninterrupted. And it paid off. Once he slowed down, he was better able to lead from a place of proactivity and peace, instead of the reactivity he didn't want. Life will surprise us, so having a plan and solid footing from which to work can be the difference between struggle and success.

After two days away, Harry went home focused. And this resulted in him doing a few things different. He did a better job planning time for his family. He started planning time for himself and got healthier. And of course, he kicked off his new CEO position with a solid ninety-day plan that impacted his first few years in that role.

The interesting thing about Harry's story is that he didn't need much help planning for his work; in reality, that came quick. What he needed was help focusing all the personal items he'd left untended. These were the items really hindering him from starting his new role strong.

The key to impact isn't doing more things. It's giving more time to the right things. Urgent things are rarely important. On the other hand, important things will never be urgent unless *you* put focus there. Little could we have known, Harry's plan was what he needed to sustain the upheaval the COVID-19 pandemic would bring just a few months after our meeting. Indeed, taking time to plan for the important helps you sustain the urgent things when they come up.

A PRINCIPLE WE'LL APPLY

If you've ever wished you had more time in the day, I've got good news. What I'm about to share could change your life. It bears repeating: *The key to impact isn't doing more things. It's giving more time to the right things. Urgent things are rarely important. On the other hand, important things are never urgent.*

Urgent things usually bear immediate consequence and are connected to *someone else's* goals. Deciding if these interruptions connect to your goals takes wisdom. Important things, however, are connected to *your* goals. Important items are things like your:

- ✔ health
- ✔ long term aspirations and vision for your organization
- ✔ your values
- ✔ most important relationships

How you treat these areas will dictate your success and satisfaction in life. And one's satisfaction (or lack thereof) shapes the way they lead. With that in mind, here's a principle to use as you take steps toward *your* most important goals.[11]

THE 80/20 PRINCIPLE

Many years ago, sociologist and economist Vilfredo Pareto noticed that eighty percent of the land in Italy was owned by twenty percent of the population. He noticed the same principle at play in other countries, too. He was curious if this principle applied to wealth as well, and it did. In other words, your most valuable assets are your twenty percent, and they dictate eighty percent of your benefits. For example, I do my best thinking in the first two hours of the workday. I use that time for deeper thinking and planning, which impacts the rest of the day. My first 20% of each day gives me 80% of my payoff. Simply put, this is the 80/20 principle. In this book, we'll think about how to apply the 80/20 principle to our time.

What if you took 20% of your work life and applied it to taking amazing care of yourself and those you lead? Like maintaining an engine, this means routine maintenance for you and those around you.

---

11   These ideas were taken from the Eisenhower Decision Matrix.

Twenty percent of your year amounts to 2.4 months. That's seventy-three days out of 365. In that time, you'll do things like vacations, planning retreats of various kinds, time with your loved ones, and other activities that will bring you life, health, and focus. If you don't take that much time currently, that's okay. You can work up to it. Developing a new habit doesn't happen overnight.

I apply this principle loosely because we each have special dynamics. Twenty percent of your work week is one day. Twenty percent of your month is about six days. Don't slice and dice your time too small. I encourage you to think in terms of planning larger chunks of time because it takes longer timeframes to do deep work and to rest. This is why these days also include the vacations you may take and some weekends.

I could never take that much time, you may be thinking. Here's the thing: you're already taking it. The data shows it. You're probably working 20% more than those you lead. Why not just get more intentional with those hours? The fact is that high-output leaders never catch up with work because there will always be more to do (like making sure others keep moving and continuous improvement). Learn to seize your strategic time. This book will help you see how.

Will you accept the fact that you're not as essential as you think? The world will go on without you. Things will be okay if you go away, just for a little while. Don't believe the lie that says results in your life or organization will only come about through your non-stop attention. Sometimes going away is the best thing you can do.

THEORY OF ACTION

As we come to the end of this introduction, I want to bring in my theory of action. I use this process when working with clients, whether they're an individual or an entire organization. Often people ask me what my program is. "Well," I say, "I don't have a program, but I do have a process." Every team, business, and market is different, so no one plan works for all. What you're about to read is a simple process by which to discern what you'll take responsibility for as a result of reading this book. By doing so, you'll also meet some specific outcomes.

In the following chapters, we'll unpack the four disciplines of retreat that will help you focus on yourself and the important people in your life. As you read, I'll have you think through the following process.

First: Listen

We each bring unique circumstances. Therefore, the content you'll discover in these pages will apply differently to each one of us. I challenge you to enter into each discipline by listening to yourself and decide what's most important for you. If you'll listen to your own issues, the outcome you'll find is your most important focus area.

Second: Find a Solution

Within each section, there will be a variety of tools mentioned and stories shared. Which tool or story seems to resonate with your being? How could the material you select be helpful to what you're noticing as you listen to body? We notice our bodies when something breaks, but what if you could listen before you ever got to that point? By choosing the right solution for your focus area, the outcome you'll find is your application point.

Third: Meet an Outcome

Notice what you'd like to see happen in your life and leadership as a result of listening and finding your chosen solution that could apply to you and/or your organization. Generalized programs rarely take root in companies because they're not contextualized. But by listening to your own dynamics, and focusing on an area specific to you, you can impact a specific outcome you need to drive.

What difference could these principles make? I encourage you to write down which strategic outcome would be most important for you to aim for at the conclusion of each section in this book. Use this as an opportunity to think higher than ground-level tactics.

THEORY OF ACTION, IN ACTION!

A few years ago, the president of a semiconductor company I know discovered a branch of the organization was about to be unionized. Picking up the phone, he called their leadership to ask what was going on. "We don't know," was their simple response. Rather than shout and tell them to figure it out, he did something I wish more leaders would do. He bought a plane ticket and flew over the ocean for a little visit.

Arriving in Ireland the following day, he went down to the factory floor and began to ask those there what was going on in the company. Despite his questioning, no one would talk.

Walking into town, he began to ask around, "What do people in Ireland do when they want to work out a problem?" What do you think they said?

The local consensus was simple and clear: "We go down to the pub!"

Walking back to the factory, the president spoke up, "All right everyone, you've got the afternoon off. I'm taking you down to the pub. Drinks on me."

Yes, this really happened.

What do you think happens when you give 300 hurt and frustrated manufacturing employees a few pints of beer each? The truth comes out. And that was the day the president discovered how underappreciated they felt. They didn't have development plans or adequate time off. They were being disrespected and talked down to. They didn't want more pay or better benefits. They wanted to be heard.

Compiling his learnings, the president went back to the leadership team and reported his findings. "The problem I found comes down to the culture of leadership you've created," he said. And after he shared what he learned, he said, "you've got six months to turn this place around or you're all gone," he said. And do you know what? Using the data compiled at the pub, and the help of a little "truth elixir," the place changed.

Was there a magic recipe for success? On the surface, all it took was one plane ticket, about a thousand dollars of beer, and a lot of listening. Was it worth it? You bet it was.

You don't get results like that with a fancy program. You get those results by listening, finding solutions to real issues, and driving an outcome that matters to real people working in the real world.

How does a leader get the confidence to behave like that? This, my friends, is where we begin. If you don't have a steady and robust interior life, it'll be hard to bring stability in the outer world. This is why our first discipline is called "Go Away Alone."

Let's get started.

O solitude! if I must with thee dwell,
Let it not be among the jumbled heap
Of murky buildings . . .
—John Keats, *"To Solitude"*

Discipline One

GO AWAY ALONE

Put this book down and set a timer for three minutes. In the quiet, breathe slow and deep. Close your eyes. Your alarm will tell you when your time is up. Go ahead.

How was that? Was it relaxing, or did it bring anxiety? What came to mind? Was it your list of action items? Your physical tiredness? Something else? What came to you isn't good or bad; it's just evidence of what's swirling around in the depths of your consciousness. I did this recently with the leader of a company and he said, "Do you want to know what my body was telling me? I noticed how I couldn't keep my legs still. It's like they were shouting at me, saying, 'We need to get up and do something!'"

The more we do this, the deeper we can go. And the deeper we go will eventually lead to what we need to notice (more on this in a moment). Why would some-one's legs be "shouting" that they had to get up and do something? There's something there. Listen.

From the time we're young, we're taught to listen to everyone but ourselves. But learning to navigate our own interior terrain is perhaps the most important skill we can ever attain. Science has shown that real inner dialogue with oneself deepens awareness of what's important.[12] Malcom Gladwell has also written that good decision-making is the result, not of more knowledge, but of understanding.[13] How well do you do with understanding yourself?

For the more technically minded, think of this through the lens of the scientific method. Plan an experiment to listen to yourself. Execute what you learn. Measure the results. Re-plan the experiment, try again. This is another way to understand what I'm saying.

Getting away alone allows you to hone this skill, get aligned with your purpose, or reconnect with the transcendent. Master Yoda once instructed a middle-aged Obi-Wan Kenobi on this topic: "Until the time is right, disappear, we will. Master Kenobi, wait a moment. In your solitude on Tatooine, training I have for you."[14]

Training in what, Master Yoda? That's just the point. You just never know when you go into solitude. It has a way of surprising us. And after the initial surprise, we can work from there. Going into the quiet with an agenda is all right. But being open to the agenda changing is the point. Slow down, embrace stillness, and see what

---

12   https://www.nature.com/articles/532032a
13   For more, see Gladwell's book, *Blink: The Power of Thinking Without Thinking*
14   Star Wars Episode Three, *Revenge of the Sith.*

happens. In the quiet, anything can come up. It could be something about yourself, your family, work, or vision for life. Sometimes it's funny how simple it is.

THE RICH INTERIOR LIFE

Near the beginning of each month, I take a few hours in solitude to think about the coming month and what I need to notice. Recently, in this time away, I was walking a trail close to my house. An idea came up that I wasn't expecting. The thought was that I needed to teach my son how to cook. *How interesting*, I thought. Bringing the thought home, I ran it by my him, and he appreciated that I was willing to give him guidance on how to make his own food since he is a picky eater (at this phase in life). Now, once a week, he makes the food he likes. It's been a huge relief to my wife. This random thought turned out to be important for our household. For me, these times of solitude bring up things about my work life, too.

Years ago, while walking this same trail, I had the idea to make some shifts in my business. I was too busy with individual coaching clients and I noticed my fatigue. *Why am I getting so tired by this?* After walking for a while, the answer came. *I enjoy deeper time with people,* I realized. *I don't need to keep packing my schedule with one-hour meetings. I could shift my work to focus more on retreats with leaders and writing.* After these thoughts came, I began to imagine what I could create around these new ideas. A few hours of quiet ended up changing a large portion of my work. That time eventually opened a new market for my business and allowed me to produce writing (including this book) that continues to bring good dividends.

Solitude matters. To not pay attention to what can only come up in the quiet runs the risk of putting you on the reactive.

In his autobiography, Nelson Mandela wrote about his first time in solitary confinement and how it almost drove him mad, even to the place where he found himself wanting to talk with a cockroach. Many years later after he was freed, he said that the impact this had on him was that he "came out mature."[15] It took twenty-seven years for Nelson Mandela to emerge a different person. And, like Mandela, someone with an aligned inner and outer life can be a force to be reckoned with.

On the other hand, when a person's inner life is compartmentalized and separate from their public work, this "allows the shadow to grow unchecked until it emerges, larger than life, in the public realm."[16] Throughout history, we've seen this dynamic play out again and again. Leaders get caught doing illegal or immoral activities. And the fallout hurts their families,

15   For more, see Nelson Mandela's Autobiography: *A Long Walk to Freedom*.

16   Palmer, Parker J. *Let Your Life Speak: Listening to the Voice of Vocation*. San Francisco, John Wiley & Sons, 2000. p. 79

colleagues, and those invested in their organization (or country). Why does this happen to so many?

Buddha once said, just as a "candle cannot burn without fire, men cannot live without a spiritual life." That's a rich metaphor. Take a moment and read it again. We westerners often miss the point of sayings from another culture and context. *What part is spiritual*, we think. *Is it the candle, the wick, or the fire?* We slice and dice things, wondering how to separate components to see how it all fits together. Thinking more broadly about the metaphor, a candle is useless without fire, and vice-a-versa. All the parts need each other. It's the same for you. All the parts of your life need each other, too.

The late literary pastor and theological writer Eugene Peterson once said that he believed the word spiritual was "cheap" because it makes people think they can "segment their lives." Rather, he said, "The whole world is spiritual, and the [Greek] word 'spirit' is 'wind.' It's 'breath [in Hebrew].' Well, people are breathing all over the place," he said, "they're all spiritual beings . . . "[17] What Peterson was saying, I believe, is that everything we do is spiritual. Everything we engage in is important and significant.

Whether or not you believe in the divine or a higher power, the point I'm trying to make is that your entire life counts. Your inner thoughts and feelings matter, just

---

17   https://onbeing.org/programs/eugene-peterson-answering-god/

as your outer work matters. Yet, the theme I've seen in my work is that many leaders are more focused on their outer work, and they don't have an inner life that can sustain their heavy workload. Therefore, paying attention to your core, and making regular time to do so, is essential. History has shown, over and over, a leader driven primarily by outside circumstances (and not their own inner compass) will, at some point, cause problems.

Expense reports get falsified.

An extramarital affair is covered up with bribe money.

Bank fraud becomes a way to make just a little extra.

Sexual misconduct takes place and lives are ruined.

"Leaders who lose their way are not necessarily bad people," writes Bill George for the Harvard Business School, "rather, they lose their moral bearings, often yielding to seductions [or distractions] in their paths."[18] Few of us went into leadership with the motivation to do wrong, but unless we understand how to build in practices that keep us from these pitfalls, the potential is always there. How can we stay grounded?

From long ago, an ancient story has been told of a man who rose to power, lost his way, went into exile, and came back to lead one of the most important nations on earth. And from his story we find much leadership wisdom. His name was Moses.

---

18   https://hbswk.hbs.edu/item/why-leaders-lose-their-way

BECOMING A PERSON WHO NOTICES

The story goes that in ancient Egypt, Pharaoh's daughter found baby Moses abandoned in a boat made of reeds floating in the Nile River. She adopted the child and raised him as her own. Moses was Jewish, but he was raised as an Egyptian.[19]

Do you know what it's like to be raised in between two worlds? I do. Being raised culturally white, but having brown skin, was a confusing experience. On one hand, I've always known English as my mother tongue. But as a teenager, growing up in east Tennessee, I was called racist names and told to "go back where I came from." Moses must have had a similar experience. He was culturally Egyptian, but racially Jewish. Who does a child talk to about that? Can you imagine the inner confusion this man must have carried?

As a young man, Moses observed a fellow Jew being mistreated by an Egyptian taskmaster. Taking matters into his own hands, he murdered the abuser and hid his body in the sand. When Pharaoh heard, he was furious, and tried to have Moses killed. But Moses ran for his life and fled into the desert.

We don't know much about Moses's early life, but we do know that he'd learned enough of his story to know that he didn't like how his people were being treated

---

19   For more, see Exodus Chapter 2

(for they were slaves). Having no one to talk to about it, his sense of justice must have become unbearable. I wonder if Moses reflected on this as he found himself in the uninhabited regions of the desert. Years of undiscerned thoughts and feelings (about his origins, race, religion, politics, and identity) had come out sideways. Did he regret his actions? Though we can never know the answer, we can know one thing for sure—the coming years in the desert were going to change him into a particular type of person.

Moses became a shepherd. Day and night, Moses's primary job was to ensure the safety of his flock. I wonder how he handled those first few years alone. Were his thoughts filled with regret? Was he happy he was out of Egypt? Whatever the case, the years in the desert slowly ground away his rough exterior. Eventually, his interior changed, too.

One day while tending his sheep, he saw a strange sight. A bush was on fire, but not burning up. Why was this? Moses decided to take a detour to go have a look. Exodus 3:4 says, "When God noticed that Moses turned aside, He called to him from within the bush."

Moses, a natural born leader, had gone astray. As a younger man, his power without character (or quiet) became aggression. Fleeing for his life, solitude was initially a hiding place. Now, many years later (about forty), solitude turned into a teacher. It took Moses four decades to become a particular kind of person—*the kind of person who noticed things.*

Exodus 3:4 could be written like this: "When God noticed that Moses had turned into the kind of person who noticed things, *then* He called to him . . . "

Are you picking up what I'm putting down? A person who does not notice things (or ignores them) is the most dangerous person in the room. I've been around too many people like this in business. We see them in politics, too. They are everywhere. Some of them come to your house for family gatherings and they destroy everything. If you break down what it is about these people, it all comes down to this: the unhealthy and unnoticed parts of a person's interior will destroy what's on the outside if not visited and healed up. But once you face your shadows, you're free. Richard Rohr writes, "Once you have faced your own hidden or denied self, there's not much to be anxious about anymore, because there is no fear of exposure—to yourself and others . . . You finally are who you are and can be who you are without disguise or fear."[20]

Fear is a significant limiting factor for leaders that causes some to delay important decisions, wait, or do nothing. Successful people, however, make choices with internal freedom. This allows objectivity with decision criteria and gets a better outcome. It is fear of failure that causes executives to cook the books and prevents people from addressing problems in their companies

20   Rohr, Richard. *Falling Upward: A Spirituality for the Two Halves of Life*. San Francisco, Jossey-Bass, 2011. p. 134

while waiting for a resolution that may not come. Face your fear, and you'll find freedom.

Fear impacts so much, even our self-presentation. When we introduce ourselves, we ask, "What's your name?" And then, "What do you do?" Just try asking someone instead, "Who are you?" I promise you'll stump most people.

If you'd asked Moses that question after forty years in the desert he probably would have answered, "I'm Moses, and I'm a quiet man who had to face some shadows. I'm the son of privilege, born a Jew, but raised Egyptian. Neglected and confused, I killed someone and ran for my life. But who am I now? I've become a person who notices things."

We don't know how many other shepherds passed the burning bush that day. But we know one thing for sure: the shepherd that got the call was the one who faced his shadows, stopped, and turned aside.

Remember Harry who didn't want to sell his soul? The great thing about Harry was that he noticed something about himself. This (in my estimation) is the most important quality for a healthy leader. Do you notice things about yourself and your environment, like your impact on others, or whether anyone is actually following you? Or are you just crashing through the world thinking you're successful because you're not being challenged?

Missing this trait will put you on the defensive for the rest of your life because you'll blame the outside world for your problems and anxieties. But by *noticing*, you'll learn to live from *your* inner conviction. This doesn't happen quick. It's a process of transformation that happens slowly across life stages. It starts when you slow down to get clear on your values and the inner work that only you can do. What kind of person do you want to be? How do you need to mature? Once you get clear there, and do your own work, you'll discover that people will follow a leader like that.[21]

Here's the good news: the path to clarity is often closer than we think. By slowing down to notice, we can learn to pay attention to one of our most valuable assets— our bodies.

LISTEN TO YOUR BODY

What I couldn't comprehend during the time of my mental breakdown was why my body shut down on me. I didn't know at the time that I'd lived for too many years on adrenaline and my body couldn't sustain it. Our bodies are like a second brain, constantly sending information to our heads. But in my non-stop mode of working, I stopped paying attention. Since then, I've

---

21 I unpack how people develop and change in my previous book, *Embrace What You Don't Know: A Stupid Guide to Smart Leadership*. For more, see Chapter 1: Creating Stability at Every Stage of Life.

learned about how the body works. In particular, the Autonomic Nervous System (ANS).

The two parts of the ANS are the sympathetic and parasympathetic nervous systems. The sympathetic drives our fight or flight responses by stimulating adrenaline and cortisol to get us ready to protect ourselves or run when there is danger. On the other hand, the parasympathetic nervous system is at work when we are relaxed.[22] This part of our ANS helps us unwind, calm down, (and as some have said) "rest and digest." Some of us are moving so fast (operating out of the sympathetic nervous system) that we're addicted to "feeling anxious and overwhelmed," not knowing that we may be "dealing with elements of disassociation."[23] This is what happened to me years ago. My kids would say "Dad, can you pass the Cheetos?" And I'd hear "chocolate burritos." They would laugh at me, but what was happening was that I was disassociated. I'd miss details in conversations and walk places, not remembering how I got there. Can you relate? Slow down for a moment and ask yourself if the phrases, "I'm doing too much," or "I'm moving too fast," resonate with you.

Michael Levine, has written for *Psychology Today* how "emotions drive 80 percent of the choices Americans

---

22 https://byjus.com/biology/difference-between-sympathetic-and-parasympathetic/
23 Kobler, Aundi, MA, LPC. *Try Softer, A Fresh Approach to Move Us out of Anxiety, Stress, and Survival Mode — and into a Life of Connection and Joy.* Carrol Stream, Tyndale House Publishers, 2020. p. 27

make, while practicality and objectivity only represent about 20 percent of decision-making." The 80/20 principle at work again. He continues that when we're hungry, angry, lonely, or tired—emotions take over 100% of the time.[24]

Most personal wealth advisors would also say that 100% objective criteria decision-making might make mathematical sense, but it often fails because personal emotions make us fail to execute. Factoring in human behavior with objective choices increases one's chances of success.

Knowing this, how is it possible to get peaceful and focused? Even getting into the state of mind to go away for a few days sometimes can seem overwhelming. Try this: Do a body scan. Start at your toes and work your way up your body. Where are you feeling stress or pain? Don't judge it as good or bad. Stop reading for a moment and just notice. Slowing down to pay attention could hold valuable clues for you.

In this moment, I notice that my wrists hurt. Maybe I should stop typing and give my hands a break. What did you notice?

---

24   https://www.psychologytoday.com/gb/blog/the-divided-mind/201207/logic-and-emotion

START NOTICING AND TRANSFORM

Recently I worked with John, the president of a large company and he was up for a promotion. His HR leader told me that he "was a little rough" around the edges and needed some coaching. Upon our first meeting, John launched into a twenty-minute monologue about all the things he was doing and needed to do. Internally, I noticed something. His monologue was making *me* uncomfortable. I wondered if he was telling me his strengths to cover his weaknesses. "John, I see you've got a lot going on," I said. "It also seems you've got a pretty good handle on the business side of your leadership. But I'm not here to talk with you about that. I'm here to help you learn to navigate what you *don't yet know how to do*."

Going with my gut, I did something I almost never do when I first meet a new coaching client. I asked his permission if it were okay to spend a few moments in silence to contemplate what was most important for him to focus on.

"Sure!" John responded enthusiastically. His response surprised me because, up to that point, he'd been talking so much. "Okay," I said. "I'll set a timer for just ninety seconds," and let's think on the question, "What's most important for us to notice, right now?"

At the conclusion of the time John responded, "It's amazing how fast that went. I'm never that quiet." From there, John told me some of his story.

John was known for his straight-shooting, no-nonsense personality. He prided himself on not playing political games. Problem was, he was exhausted and working thirteen hours a day. "Sure, I'm compensated well," John said, "but at what cost?"

From there, John shared about the loss of a family member and its emotional cost to his wife, who was battling some personal problems. "We're going to counseling," he said, "because it's impacted our marriage."

I asked John what it was like to have such power in the business world, but to find himself feeling powerless in his personal life. "It's extremely frustrating," he said. "In the business world, I pull and push levers and things happen. But in my personal life, it's not working that way."

"What are you learning about your growth areas from your marriage that could apply to your leadership in the company?" I asked. After a long pause, he said, "It's not often I get stumped with a question." More silence followed. "I don't know," he reiterated. I pushed gently and asked, "What if you did?"

John answered emphatically, "I'm learning that I'm not very good at taking the time to understand. In fact, when there's any ambiguity, I jump in, take over, and direct." John finally noticed something. So we started there.

We began creating a plan for John to notice what was going on in himself internally. He stopped directing and pronouncing so much and learned to ask more questions. At first it was hard, even awkward. Asking questions is a vulnerable tool for many leaders to learn because you just don't know what people are going to say. But I've seen repeatedly that leaders who master this tool win the hearts of their people. This is what happened to John.

Within a few months, John became a mentor-like figure who thoughtfully jotted down questions before meetings. He began listening before he asked anything. At first, this confused his colleagues. He began doing this at home too and started taking time to "turn aside," to write down his thoughts, and discern what the best course of action was. Rather than charging into each work or personal situation with a show of power, he learned to enter in with calm and questions. His teams grew healthier, his working relationships got an upgrade, and his marriage improved too. John began taking more time away from work to focus on himself. And a strong leader transformed into a powerful guide.

KNOW YOUR VALUES, STAND FOR YOUR NEEDS

One of the first things I do when I work with leaders is help them determine their values. From there, I encourage them to take regular time away in solitude to make sure their lives are aligned with their values, and then to reflect on how those values impact the way they lead in their organizations.

One of John's values was personal improvement. As he got clear in this, he saw the value of taking time off from work for shorter periods, even for a walk. He used this time to plan for various items of importance to him. Whether it was planning for difficult meetings, or designing special time to spend with his wife, he began to do what he needed to do for *himself*.

Remember, John was up for a promotion. This opportunity initially looked attractive but brought considerable stress. "I don't like the organization dangling this carrot in front of me," he said. When I inquired into what he meant, he said, "I want to improve for myself for me, not because someone else wants me to get promoted . . . "

As John began paying attention to his interior life, something unexpected happened. He decided he was content to keep his current role, and he briefly considered a sabbatical from work. Taking the promotion wasn't necessary for him. With this realization, he decided to pause and be okay internally if the role were to go to someone else.

"How much money is enough?" he asked me. "I've realized I have all I'll ever need. I'm not going to keep chasing success. I realize now that I've already got it."

John learned to pay attention to the health of his interior life in order to be at his best. He slowed down. He became the kind of person who noticed things. This improved many areas of his life and work. John optimized his outcomes and I'm proud to know he's making a difference.

To an ignorant ambitious person, this may look like a failure. But what would the outcome have been if John had pursued a promotion he wasn't ready for and didn't have the time or space to do well?

A MACHINE FOR MAKING MONEY

There's blatant belief in our culture that we should pay attention more to what others want for us than what we genuinely need. In fact, sometimes when we speak for our needs, we are even ridiculed. The more you live from your values, the more comfortable you get with your inner worth (apart from what you can produce). You also will begin to gain clarity to evaluate if your organization is aligned with what's important to you. The reason this is important is that no one else is in your seat—you are. That means if you're going to sustain your work for the long-term, you've got to do it your way. Don't be too busy to take care of yourself.

Muir once said, "I am losing precious days. I am degenerating into a machine for making money. I am learning nothing in this trivial world of men. I must break away and get out into the mountains to learn the news." As noted earlier, for Muir, going to the mountains was "going home." He knew that his value was beyond his work. He needed space to rest and take deep breaths; we all do. You're worth more than the profit you generate.

For you, it may not be the mountains. It may be walking around the neighborhood or choosing to engage in an activity that calms you down and brings you life or focus. Don't neglect your health, interests, and important relationships for the sake of your career. You are more valuable than your ability to generate money for shareholders. Slow down and reclaim your value as a human. To not do so will make you vulnerable to engaging in shadow missions of various sorts. Be careful. As a human, you have guiding values that will help you stay healthy. Have you made time to get clear on yours?

To get clarity on your values and live from them, you have to stop participating in the rush, just for a little while. My hope is that by doing so, you'll gain something to offer others from a place of wholeness instead of a place of emptiness. The cautionary tale I've seen many times is a leader comes to others with deficiency and demands they fill his lack.

MEETING YOUR UNMET NEEDS

Our shadow is the underside of a genuine need that's gone unmet. Some of us have gone with needs unmet for years. And rather than feel those losses, we just worked harder. But those needs don't just disappear; instead, they follow us around, just like a shadow.

Work, travel, eating, and drinking can all be acceptable cover-ups in our culture for undealt-with emotional pain. If you're an overly responsible leader, you may come from a past where you didn't have someone to stand up for you. This created the type of person who gets stuff done and stands up for others, but maybe not for yourself. Working harder may be a cover-up to avoid feeling pain. But when you don't feel, you don't deal with it. And not dealing with pain sets us up for addictive behaviors.

People-pleasing is an addiction. Co-dependency is an addiction. And there are many more. We often think of addicts as those who have a chemical dependency (like alcohol or various drugs). But an addict is anyone who needs something outside of themselves to feel okay inside. Two words can help you know if you're living from the shadows: unhealthy and unsafe. This is why burnout eventually follows.

I write these words because I've lived it. My tight schedule and overly responsible behaviors are coping skills that became maladaptive. I used these skills to control life when what I really needed was to accept life on life's terms. Today, I'm actively in various forms of recovery to feel the pain from my past and deal with the feelings that accompany the pain.

When I was a teenager, my response to my painful childhood was drugs and alcohol. In college my addictive behavior shifted to religion. Then in my young adult and professional years, it shifted to people pleasing. Then, in marriage, it was co-dependency. Then, when kids came along, my behavior shifted to the buzz that came from a savior-complex as I confidently believed I'd break a generational cycle in my family. I also built multiple iterations of my business and moved my family all over the country. I'm not proud of this paragraph. But it was the road I had to travel to face the fact that I was trying to outrun my own pain. I looked ambitious at first, but my shadows showed me I was just hurting. I'm grateful that I've learned a lot about this through my faith, in counseling, various retreats, and twelve-step meetings. If you identify with anything I've just written, maybe it's time you get help, too.

No matter who we are, we're made to be in relationship. This means we're wired to both give and receive four A's: Affection, Approval, Affirmation, and Attention.[25] Your values are ways of claiming that you will live in such a way that these four A's will be part of your life.

A shadow mission is an attempt to get our needs met, but we do it from a place of emptiness and in secret, which can really be an act of self-hatred. Here's why: when we're unable to speak for our needs in the real world with the people in our lives, going and getting it somewhere else can be a way to cover up the shame

---

25 I learned about the four A's at a professionals intensive at The Bridge to Recovery in Bowling Green, Kentucky. These four areas have also been written about in other places.

we carry with us and reinforce the brokenness of our normal life.

The word *integrity* means "whole." In other words, an integrous person is someone whose healthy inner life matches their outer one. People who live in integrity don't need to take on shadow missions because they're already doing the work to meet their needs in healthy and safe ways. Are you living in integrity?

In organizations, one's shadow values (unmet needs) are revealed when a leader behaves in unhealthy and unsafe ways contrary to company values. For example, in 2021, the CEO of Sony abruptly left to "go in a new direction." However, his leaving came on the heels of allegations of decades-long[26] bullying and harass-ment.[27] Why does a bully behave that way? Sometimes it's because they were once bullied, and other times its their way of covering up other kinds of pain. Whatever the case, every human has a need for those four A's. If we don't get our needs met, they will eventually come out in private, and sometimes become public.

In the workplace, what we often perceive as interper-sonal conflict can be someone's shadows becoming public. In Sony's case, two of their values are Integrity

---

26   https://www.abc.net.au/news/2021-10-11/facing-the-music:-the-sony-music-scandal/13579828

27   https://www.news.com.au/finance/work/leaders/sony-music-australia-ceo-and-chairman-denis-handlin-departs-company-abruptly/news-story/b77efe3c432e67fd048b842e9b5ba3c5

and Sincerity. Bullying was contrary to those values. So they let a valuable leader go.

If you identify with any of what I've just written about, it is worth the time and money to get some help. If you're still in doubt, take sixty seconds to look in the mirror and just say these words: "I'm worthy of love. I'm a worthwhile investment. Living a life of integrity and peace is possible for me." If you struggle with that exercise, it may be a sign that you don't yet believe it. Please read the following words carefully: You can change. You can feel your feelings. They won't kill you. A healthy and safe life can be yours. You owe it to yourself and those you lead.

A shadow value may be at play when you seek a solution that can't provide an answer to your true goals or needs. For instance, sometimes I feel hungry, when I'm actually dehydrated; I go for a snack when really I need water. Another example is when a person thinks they crave sex when what they really need is to be known and noticed. In this case, a potential shadow value emerges as comfort (or relief from anxiety). But was the pursuit of sex healthy and safe for your partner? If not, it came from the shadows. The real value needed is intimacy. This happens in the business world, too.

Take Volkswagen's "Dieselgate" fiasco of 2015. Volkswagen's quest to become the world's largest automaker led engineers to secretly override the emissions controls on board its diesel vehicles. They sold 11 million cars worldwide fitted with a so-called "defeat device," a mechanism installed to detect when a vehicle's emissions were being tested. But when not being tested, these vehicles violated environmental standards.[28] Volkswagen became the world's largest auto maker years ahead of schedule, but they did it from the shadows.

In Volkswagen's quest to be the biggest and greatest, they created a dangerous world. To find an organization's shadow values, start by looking at its unsafe and unhealthy practices. For Volkswagen, I wonder if we could call Dieselgate the rotten fruit of a shadow value—power without care. Who was at fault? Maybe bosses were bullies and engineers feared reporting real results. I'm sure it was complex. Whatever the case, standards were violated, and that wasn't good.

Volkswagen's big misstep led to major lawsuits and the loss of billions in 2016,[29] which forced them rethink their values. Today, they have a stated value of Responsibility. "We take on social responsibility," their website states. "We pay attention to the environmental capability of our products and processes and improve them, every day."[30]

When people and companies realize they've been

---

28   https://www.bbc.com/news/business-34324772
29   https://www.caranddriver.com/news/a15339250/everything-you-need-to-know-about-the-vw-diesel-emissions-scandal/
30   https://www.volkswagenag.com/en/group/volkswagen-group-essentials.html

living in the shadows and come clean, they make a leap toward integrity. For Volkswagen, being the biggest came with responsibility. I'm glad they chose the planet. For people, finding value clarity can help you determine what your needs are and how to be responsible to take care of yourself, creating a life of health and safety.

HOW TO FIND YOUR VALUES

There are a few ways to get clear on what's most important to you and begin to meet those needs. The easiest is to notice when you hold your breath or double gulp. These behaviors are signals that something significant to you is being trampled on. What situations bother you or make you uncomfortable? By reflecting on and exploring these circumstances, you'll uncover themes that represent a value.

A second way to discern your values is to look back on your life and notice the types of decisions you've made that you're most proud of. Often, we come to life with words and goals that have no rooting in who we actually are. Then we try to live up to those values. Instead, what if you looked at your life to see what kind of truths you already embody? Living up to these ideals is something you've always done. Find the words, and you'll strengthen the best of who you actually are.

My favorite way to unearth values is to see when a person has felt most alive or (on the other hand) experienced the most pain. This is a kind of "highs" and "lows" exercise that underscores when a person's values have been present or absent. What words do each of your highs and lows represent? Distill those to 3–5 words. What you'll find is a set of guiding behaviors you've always lived by. If some of those values are absent in your current life, this could represent a special focus area for you.

The wise Henri Nouwen once said that "in order to be of service to others, we have to die to them." Psychologists call this healthy differentiation. It's about knowing where you begin and end and the space where others also begin and end. It's about having clarity on who you are and what work takes precedent (for yourself first, then the organization) and then calling others to step in to help engage in a way that brings impact.

MY VOCATION AND VALUES

The way I discovered my values was by going away alone. It wasn't intentional at first; it was forced upon me. In my mid-thirties, I found myself restarting my career and grasping for how to do that. I'd moved my family across the country to start over and had a short timeline to make something happen. At first, I did a lot of personal reflection and walking in my neighborhood. But at some point, I discovered I needed help. I found it in various trainings and certification courses on this subject. I hired coaches, too, and put in the work to reflect on my life. What I discovered was my real vocation and my guiding values.

Your vocation is what you'd do even if you didn't get paid for it, and it transcends any job you'll ever hold. For me, I've worked a lot of jobs. In high school, I loved the interaction I had with new people while I waited tables and worked in retail. In college, I uncovered my own creativity working as a landscaper. Later, working at a record store, I found joy in music and the arts. Eventually, I discovered my knack for teaching and leadership in my church and at summer camps. As an adult, I've applied my interest in people, creativity, and leadership in many ways as a high school teacher, pastor, a coach, and consultant.

In my previous book, *Embrace What You Don't Know*, I shared how I was raised in an environment of screaming and fighting. Despite the damage this caused, this upbringing taught me the importance of emotional health, listening to understand, and the value of talking straight. I also shared how I lived a life without purpose and how a profound faith conversion changed things for me. Now I work toward helping others see a broader purpose for their lives and work. My vocation, or calling, can be reduced to one simple idea: creatively guiding people to lead from a higher cause. Reflecting on it, no matter what job I've ever had, I've always created conversations around this subject.

In terms of my values, I've got four. I've been most fulfilled when I:

1. Had the **COURAGE** to change.

2. Maintained good relational **CONNECTION** to others

3. Lived from a place of **HONESTY**

4. Stayed true to my **HEART** and aligned with a higher cause

When I've been most embarrassed or unhappy has always been connected to the times when I veered off course from these values. My own development pathway involves putting things right when I miss the mark and getting close to others who embody these values also so I can continually deepen in maturity. Remember those four A's from earlier? As I work to get aligned with my values, I find I get the Affection, Approval, Affirmation, and Attention I need. I also get better at giving those things, too.

Your unique life's work and values are found in your story. Have you spent the time to dig in to find those words? Many are too busy to do this work and shelve it for another time when life will be less hectic. But my experience has taught me that there's never a convenient time to do important work. You've got to make it.

HOW I STAY ALIGNED

As mentioned earlier, I clear a few hours at the beginning of each month to take a long walk in the quiet (no phone, no people) to reflect on my work and values. How am I doing? Where am I strong? Where am I off track? As I walk, I spend time attending to what I notice. Remember the primary quality of healthy leadership? I've got to make space to notice things. If I don't, how can I be of any use to others? The more I do this, the more others see how to do it, too. The result is that I'm surrounded by people who also notice things about themselves and clear the space to grow in their lives.

When I return from these walks, I take about an hour to look over my month and schedule items pertaining to what I noticed. Sometimes this means making more time for my wife or kids. Other times it results in taking healthy and calculated risks at work with the people I lead. Often, it means taking things *out* of my schedule that are misaligned with my vocation and values.

The neat thing about this exercise is that it began more as a tool by which to evaluate and critique my life. But as this habit has deepened, it's turned more into an exercise of communion with myself, with nature, and with my higher power.

I wasn't always this way. As a younger man, I filled my time with people, meetings, and emails. I believed I always needed to be "on." But, as I shared earlier, that way of behaving led to my demise. I'm grateful I've emerged more focused and intentional. It's brought me a lot of peace.

HOW YOU CAN GO AWAY ALONE

If you think your work is currently too urgent to allow time for this kind of values clarification and noticing, then do it over the course of a weekend. If you have more autonomy at work, clear time during your work week. If you still think are too busy to do this, you might be living from potential shadow values that could drive you to unhealthy approval or creating false security. We each know deep inside that we've got an inner compass we need to listen to. Learning to live from a healthy place where we notice these things is essential.

Once you've found clarity on your values using one of the exercises I shared earlier, then clear some time monthly to reflect on how aligned you are. Adjust your schedule to keep you on track. The clearer you are on your values and work, the more you'll look forward to these times. Living from your values ensures you'll become more of who you've always been. Others will see you do it and wonder if they can live this way also. Who wouldn't want to be surrounded by friends, family, leaders, and teams like that?

Taking time to go away alone is an important first discipline. Unfortunately, when a person hasn't done this in little bits throughout their lives, sometimes greater steps have to be taken. Extended breaks are great. However, if you've been taking time along the way to live from your values, such extreme measures probably won't be necessary for your survival. Instead, extended breaks can become times of rest and relaxation.

We humans view the ceasing of work as death. But as you make space to be quiet and, perhaps take some extended time in nature, you'll see that (in nature) death is always the foundation of a new beginning.

SUMMARY

🔊 Listen

As you think about taking time away to become *a particular kind of person*, one who notices things, what comes up for you?

_____

_____

_____

_____

🔍 Find a Solution

How might you address your values, or governing objectives? Pay attention, these will help you prioritize action. Are you aligned or misaligned with those values? What about being a person who notices things, how do you do with that? How might your inner life be impacting the life of your team or organization? How much (or little) time do you take per month to check-in with yourself and your inner life? Is that enough for where you're currently at in life?

✏️ Meet an Outcome

Based on what's come up for you, which item seems to be of most importance? If you'd address it, what effect do you think that would have?

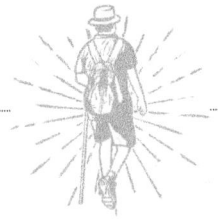

"Yesterday I was clever, so I wanted to change the world. Today I am wise, so I am changing myself."

—Rumi

Discipline Two

GO AWAY
WITH
A GUIDE

From ancient Greek mythology, we learn the cautionary tale of Narcissus. He was very attractive and had many female admirers. At a young age, it was prophesied that he could stop himself from growing old—if he resisted the temptation to look at his reflection. Narcissus was in a predicament. He wondered what he looked like but remembered the prophecy. He withdrew from others and returned love to no one.

One day, a young nymph named Echo spotted Narcissus in the woods. Echo had been cursed by the goddess Hero, so that she could only repeat the sounds and words of others. She fell in love with Narcissus and followed him for days until he turned and caught her. Echo tried to embrace him, but Narcissus rejected her since she only mimicked his voice. Brokenhearted, she ran into the forest, and eventually died (her spirit echoing on in the rocks, and trees, and water). Day after day, Narcissus wandered in the forest, hearing her whisper (which sounded just like him).

One day while hunting, he came across a pool of water. Looking in, he saw his reflection and became infatuated with himself. Over time, he returned again and again to see his reflection. It became one his favorite things to do. Each day he stared longer and longer. Eventually, he wasted away and died while looking at his image.[31]

The lesson in this story is this: Too much time in your own head can be a problem.

Have you ever known a "narcissistic" leader? They seem absorbed in themselves, and what others think which hinders them from reaching outcomes. But imagine what could happen if they'd listen to outside wisdom? What if we all had people surrounding us that were beyond us in age, maturity, or experience? Imagine the clarity that could bring.

The higher you go in leadership, the less people will tell you the truth, so surrounding yourself with trusted advisors is essential. It's lonely at the top, but it doesn't have to be. Earlier, I mentioned my ecosystem of wisdom. This is the group of people who make up my advisors. They are the mentors and coaches who help guide my work, keep me out of my head, and help me create the kind of life (and work) I want. In this section, I'll tell you about some of them.

Who is in your ecosystem?

---

31   There are many versions of this story. For more see: https://www. historicmysteries.com/narcissus-myth-version-poets/

TWO IMPORTANT HELPERS

There are two kinds of people you'll want in your ecosystem: mentors and coaches.

A mentor is someone you may or may not pay. They are probably beyond you in life stage (and age) whom you may consult for guidance and friendship. They'll probably share a fair bit of their experience and perspective with you. And, depending on their place in life, they may give you their time for free. Some may charge you, depending on the situation. On the other hand, a coach is a paid guide who designs an agenda based on self-discovery around your goals and questions. Where a mentor may be limited in time, a coach can come in to do more intensive work with you. We need both.

In the first part of this chapter, I want to share why mentors are so important. And briefly, in the last part, I'll share how this can impact your work and how a coach may help take you further. I'd like to begin by introducing you to one of my mentors, Joe.

Joe helps lead a global faith-based non-profit. He's also an artist, a former pastor, and teacher. For a few years now, I've asked Joe for mentoring in the area of character, life-stage development, and clarifying my vocation. To give you a window in on my work with him, I'd like to take you back a few years to a cold winter day where I sat by a warm fire in his living room.

I'd made the journey to Joe's house on Oconomowoc Lake in Wisconsin to explore questions about calling. "I feel like I've lost my passion," I said. "I've done a lot of things, and am still *doing* a lot of things, but for some reason I'm not looking forward to any of it. I've gone through some hard stuff and life seems to be rebuilding, but I feel alone, and I don't really care about much of it."

Joe opened the front of the fireplace, inserted another log, and said, "Sometimes running out of ourselves is the greatest gift we can ever get." He sat back down and remained quiet.

Okay, I thought.

I waited for more as I watched the snow fall outside. *What's he going to say next?* I wondered.

After about thirty seconds of silence. Joe gathered his thoughts and continued. "When we are stripped of our familiar comforts and people who flatter us, it's for our own well-being. Something's happening right now *in* you," he observed.

Good conversations start with great listening, and on that day, I needed to be heard. In the years following my mother's death, I'd rebuilt my business and moved my family across the country. But something was lacking. Joe helped me understand that I'd been organizing the chess pieces of my life for a long time and it had exhausted me. My next phase of development would be more focused on my internal life. Later on that trip,

Joe inspired me to think more about working on myself. "You're in an important time of character development," he said. "Be patient."

Those days were the beginning of me recovering some passion in my life. I've learned a lot since then, too, but I couldn't have seen it without a mentor.

Who do you have in your life that will speak to you with such thoughtfulness?

WHY YOU NEED A GUIDE

Going away with a mentor can help you clarify your passion and your calling. The word *passion* (in Latin) means "to suffer." Looking back on it now, what I was really asking at that time was, "What's worth suffering for?" What I've learned since then is that the thing worth suffering for is calling—this idea that my unique story and truths can be manifested in certain works in this world. Yet sometimes, my calling can get buried beneath all the clutter in my mind.

In his classic work, *East of Eden*, John Steinbeck wrote about his perspective on what happens in the mind of a man. "Our species is the only creative species," he wrote, "and it has only one creative instrument, the individual mind and spirit of man. Nothing was ever created by two men. There are no good collaborations . . . "

There is so much depth in this thought, yet so much self-defeating philosophy. I agree that within many of us, there's an original idea, and working towards unearthing it is important. But for the rest of us, we need help honing our thoughts and making sense of what we want to focus on in a world packed with information. Even the most brilliant people have needed mentors. To think that there are no good collaborations just isn't true. Collaborative partnerships take many forms. Mentoring is one.

Here are a few famous mentoring relationships you may or may not be aware of.

Steve Jobs once mentored Mark Zuckerberg on how to stay connected to his original mission. Warren Buffet mentored Bill Gates on how to think differently about Microsoft. Oprah Winfrey called Maya Angelou one of the greatest influences in her life and learned from Angelou how to build trust and relationships.

It may be time for a mentor when you just can't see what's next or are having trouble focusing. Maybe your calling is unclear, and you need a voice of wisdom to help you see it. "Calling is tricky," Joe told me once, "because it transcends anything we will ever produce. It's more about what we carry inside of us, despite what we ever can do."

There's a lot in that statement that bears repeating— in particular, that your life's work is about more than

your day job. It's about the sculpting of your character and a kind of "coming home" to your true nature.
When we're clear on that, the suffering that comes is
somehow more bearable. An important note—calling
isn't always fulfilling because it sometimes involves a
lot of waiting. Yet, the waiting is worth it because work
that's aligned with your calling (for those of us who get
clear here) may not even feel like work. I didn't find this
clarity overnight. It happened through many conversations with the right mentors. Though I've gravitated
intuitively toward a certain kind of person to guide
me, I've developed a more systematic approach to
finding mentors as I've grown older. In a few moments,
I'll share how I do it and how I encourage my clients to
do it as well. But first, let's go deeper with some more
signs that you might be ready for a mentor.

GO AWAY WITH A MENTOR

The proactive signs might be a desire to grow and
mature as you age, or as your career changes. As I've
done retreats with clients, I've seen how some need an
internal check-in, a little rest, or help planning their next
quarter, or year. And though these practical steps may
be better suited to a coaching relationship, a mentor
can help in these areas, too. You may be unsure of
where to focus next, given the demands on your time.
With a good mentor, you can find focus and take that
focus further with the help of a coach.

The reactive signs that you may need to find a mentor are a little different. Some leaders have "monkey mind."[32] You may feel scattered and easily distracted, unable to prioritize what's truly important. You may feel your heart racing or pulse pounding as you struggle to get clarity. Others feel fatigue or experience other bodily signs that they need a reset. Another indicator that you need a mentor is if you've received negative feedback about your job performance. Worse yet would be if you haven't received *any* feedback because your team perceives you as unsafe or unresponsive. Like Narcissus, too much time in the weeds of your own thoughts can take you out.

Bob Iger, CEO of Disney, explained that one of the reasons he left his role in 2021 was that, over time, he tolerated other people's opinions less and less. "That was an early sign that it was time," he said. "Look, the world is changing dramatically, and it's important for the CEO of a company to address all of those changes rapidly."[33] He knew that if he was going to address change, he also needed to be a person who was willing to change. That's wisdom. Iger ended up returning to Disney less than a year later to help bring the company into a season of new growth. But with a leader who will go away when he notices something about himself that needs attention, I bet Disney will keep doing great.

---

32 https://www.stress.org/please-meet-your-monkey-mind
33 https://www.cnbc.com/amp/2021/12/21/disney-chairman-bob-iger-explains-why-hes-leaving-the-company.html

Do you want to get better? A book will help, and time alone is good. But time with an older mentor is really where it's at. Going to their home turf and watching how they live will broaden your horizons, too. As St. Augustine said, "The world is a book and those who do not travel read only one page." Your work is full of complexities. Expanding your view and changing locations is a great way to equip yourself to meet the ever-changing landscape of your responsibilities.

Who comes to your mind when you think of someone who brings a different outlook in age, industry, maturity, and wisdom? What would it look like for you to reach out and schedule a conversation?

CHANGE YOUR MIND ABOUT INDIVIDUALISM

If you're like me, you may accept the need for a relationship like this, but not make the time. I didn't always make time for mentors; I grew into it by necessity.

I was formed in an environment that taught me that if anything was going to get done, I had to do it. Trust no one, and take on leadership of everything to ensure it happens right and on time. For a long time, my life motto was "work harder and move faster." And though I still struggle with a superman mentality, at least I'm aware of it now.[34] It's just plain false for anyone to think that you got to where you are entirely on your own.

You weren't born independently. At a minimum, you were birthed by your mother. You didn't find nourishment independently either. This fact remains as long as you live, and we're reminded of it multiple times a day when we get hungry. We need outside strength to keep on going. Speaking of food, most people don't realize that their vegetables travel thousands of miles just to get to the grocery store. What about the farmers, truck drivers, grocery store workers, and many others? To think you are an island is just plain ignorant. You need others. Most don't realize that our idolization of rugged American individualism keeps us lonely, ignorant, and unhappy. Could it be that we love Steinbeck's "lonely genius" idea because it's the culture we're immersed in?

I had to realize this the hard way. During my mental breakdown, though it was confusing to lose the ability to do the things I once did, it taught me to reach out for help. I was like Narcissus, lost in my thoughts and ideas. As a younger man, I just couldn't see it. Now, in my mid-40s, I'm starting to see outside myself. Mentors have helped, but it wasn't just about the answers they gave. Their real value was

---

34 This is what Impostor Syndrome looks like, and many executives struggle with it. Dr. Valerie Young has written extensively on this in her book, *The Secret Thoughts of Successful Women: Why Capable People Suffer From the Imposter Syndrome and How to Thrive in Spite of It.* In her writing, she outlines five types of impostor syndrome scenarios. 1. The Perfectionist, 2. The Superwoman/man, 3. The Natural Genius, 4. The Soloist, 5. The Expert.

bringing new perspectives I hadn't thought of. This led to new ideas, solutions, and goals within me.

Rugged individualism may help you survive the Oregon Trail, but it won't help you develop healthy relationships, or magnify your impact, which comes from the work of an engaged team. Your team needs healthy relationships as does your family (both items we'll talk about in the subsequent chapters of this book). We're interdependent people, which means we need to lean on the right relationships at the right time. Though I have multiple mentors like Joe now, I built up to it. Here's how I do it.

HOW I FIND MENTORS

The psychologist Carl Jung believed our hidden and best self could be found in our secret dislikes, as well as in our deepest admirations. To find your own lifetime development pathway, I guide my clients in the following exercise.

Think of a person (or people) whose behavior you dislike. What qualities about them bother you? Write their name on the left side of the following chart and all the qualities you can think of. Now think of a person (or people) that you admire. What qualities about them do you hope to integrate into your life the older you get? Write down all their qualities that you can think of as well.

Circle the qualities on the left that you absolutely disdain. Also, now circle the qualities on the right that you admire the most.

List below the names of people you don't like very well (or at least, they bother you).	List below the names of people you admire.
List below the negative qualities of these people. When you finish, circle the qualities you find despicable.	**List the wonderful qualities of these people. When you finish, circle the qualities you deeply admire or envy.**

What you're looking at on the left side of the chart may point to behaviors about yourself you do not like. If that's true, what do these behaviors teach you about yourself?

What you're looking at on the right may point to character qualities you once had that you need to embrace
more fully. If that's not true for you, why do you admire
the qualities on the right side of the chart? How could
your life and leadership be impacted if you'd more fully
grow into those qualities? How could you more fully
enter into a phase of development with one of those
people on the right side of the chart?

If you listed the same person for both columns, this
could point to someone who is very much like you, both
in behaviors you dislike and in admirable qualities. If
this seems true for you, you might engage them in a
conversation about how they are able to carry traits
that seem in opposition.

My mentors have come from names I've scribbled in the
right column.[35] What about you? Consider your growth
needs and find someone who can journey with you.

After I've identified a potential mentor, I reach out and
tell them what I'm hoping for. From there, I ask if they
are open to spending some time together. Ideally, I fly to
them for a few days and this gets me out of the details
of my daily grind. It also provides a fresh perspective

---

35   This exercise was created and adapted from William A. Miller's
book, *Make Friends with Your Shadow*, Augsburg Fortress Pub, 1981.
Also see Janet Hagberg's book *Real Power: Stages of Personal Power
in Organizations*, Scheffield Publishing, 2003. Chapter 12, *Leading from
Your Soul*, expands on the concept of consulting your shadows by also
looking at your childhood wounds.

I can take home. Getting away together sometimes provides a space for the rest I need. Plus, it's fun.

From my experience, they usually say yes. Only once has someone turned me down, an older man in his eighties. His reason was simple: "I'm getting older and I want to focus on writing in my latter years of life," he explained. I respected his decision, and it made sense. Yet, in that instance, his turning me down led me to seek out someone else, another lifelong mentor named Ron who works on the campus of UC Berkeley. Ron helped me survive graduate school and has been a consistent voice of guidance for nearly twenty-five years now. At times, someone you pursue may be focused on other goals, and that's all right. Use the opportunity to find another person who is more available.

As I've pursued mentors for many years now, I've found another surprising biproduct. As my network expands to include that of my mentors, I meet others who are curious about this kind of relationship. This has led younger leaders from my mentors' networks to ask me for guidance. It's fun to have these new faces come to visit me for a few days, not to mention what an honor it is.

I've found mentors by accident, too. In my case, after my mental breakdown, I was desperate for help. And though I didn't know where to look, my radar was up for help, and it came from an unexpected place. One day while at a conference, I overheard a colleague talking about a spiritual director she had worked with. I had never worked with a spiritual director and wondered what this was about. When I inquired, I learned about Father Len, who ran a retreat center outside Boston. I called Len, who was in his mid-sixties, and we began regular phone conversations. Months later, while in Boston for work with a company, I decided to take extra time to go to Worcester (pronounced "Woostah"), where he lives.

During that visit, I got to watch how Len lived. I saw how he cared for his wife (who was dying and has since passed away), how he opened his home, how he held meetings with groups, and how he prayed. My relationship with Len on his home turf showed me what a strong, mature, and selfless man looked like. And our relationship has continued for a few years now.

That same timeframe was when I met Joe (who I mentioned earlier) on a business trip. At the time, Joe seemed very busy. But a wise leader told me once "never say no for someone." So rather than assuming Joe wouldn't have the time, I asked him if we could get some time together and then allowed him to make the choice. I'm grateful he said yes.

Joe, Ron, and Len are three of the mentors in my world that I admire, and they admire me. They've helped me see my own blind spots, make plans for my life, and supported me along the way. I'm thankful for them and the others who have invested in me.

My younger self didn't value relationships as much I do now. But, as Gerald O'Collins has written, quoting Carl Jung, "We cannot live the afternoon of life according to the program of life's morning: for what in the morning was true will at evening have become a lie."[36] In other words, what got you here won't get you there. You are changing as you age. Your practices must also.

It's commonly said that insanity is doing the same thing over and over expecting a different result. If you're still reading, you probably have an inclination that you need to try something new. Why not go away with a mentor? Just imagine how you, your family, or your organization could benefit.

PREPARING FOR TIME AWAY

Depending on your life season, you may choose to go away to spend time with a mentor, coach, or other guide. I recommend my clients go away at least once yearly (preferably twice) for a 36-48 hour on-the-ground retreat, at a minimum. Our first retreat is usually around alignment of their values in their lives and then how they use their voice within their organization. From there, we can work on other items. I help them prepare in four ways.

---

36   O'Collins, Gerald. *The Second Journey: Spiritual Awareness and the Mid-Life Crisis.* New York, Paulist Press, 1987. p. 4

First: Block Off the Time in Advance

If you have an assistant, utilize their help to select the best time. Remember that what's important is rarely urgent, so plan to make this time a priority. When you get closer to the date, something urgent *will* come up. Decide in advance to keep this time, no matter what.

When the time for your trip comes, what do you need to delegate so you can fully calm down, focus, and do the deep work? Remember, to transform our organizations, it requires making the space for ourselves to transform. You'll also be able to guide others in a process if you yourself are continually practicing it. That's an important part of your job, by the way. There's the work (vision, strategy, tactics), and then there's the work *of* a leader. The work of a leader is to help others develop and grow.

Second: Be Clear on Your Unique Voice & Values

As mentioned in Chapter One, your values (or governing tenants) are what's most important to you. Not living true to those behaviors will bother you because an important need in your life will go unmet which could create lack of health and safety for you, and others. So going into a retreat being clear here is vital. Sometimes it takes months to get clear on these items; spend time with a coach beforehand so when the trip comes, you're prepared.

The result: when you're clear on your values, you can use your voice to advocate for them. Remember, your voice comes from your unique story, which will transcend any job you'll ever have. One way to find clarity on your voice is to think about what makes you angry. I'm angry when I see lack of leadership depth and character. I'm also angry about depression, racism, and cerebral palsy. These things aren't unique to me (though this combination may be). But what makes them unique is that they are rooted in my experience, so I'm passionate to do something about them. My voice comes from my emotions and thoughts about these issues.

Third: Assess Your Life & Leadership

An easy way to gain awareness on areas in your life and leadership is to utilize a life and/or leadership assessment wheel. Do an internet search and you'll find many examples of wheels that can help you rate your health in various areas of life, like purpose, relationships, finances, physical health, and work.[37] For leadership-specific wheels, you can rate yourself on culture-change, coaching, or communication (among other items).[38]

Find a wheel that works for you and rate yourself from 1–10 in each area. If a ten is perfect, which areas are high

---

37 https://positivepsychology.com/wheel-of-life-coaching/
38 https://dhsleadup.oucpm.org/2016/09/get-prepared-for-session-five-pre-class-assignments/

for you? How does that point to the values you embody best? In the low areas, how does that point to what you need to take away from this retreat? If the wheels you utilize don't contain an important category for you, which would you add? How would you rate yourself? Why is that important?

Fourth: Plan to Have Fun & Recharge

Sit-down meetings will only do so much and can get tiring, so plan to have fun. Some clients (like Harry from earlier) opt to do something fast and active like mountain biking. Others like to take it slow with extended walks. For me, on a retreat with clients, I use these active times to reflect on the work of the morning, have fun, and get to know one another better. If you need some quiet time, plan for a nap or a massage. It's your time. What would it take for you to want to do this regularly? If your retreat lasts longer than 24 hours, go deeper with items that came up in day one on the second day. After my clients look at their lives on day one, they often opt to shift to organizational goals on day two.

MY FIRST GUIDE

My approach to leadership development looks like this because the work of leading is fundamentally relational. But I didn't always think this way. My philosophy began its formation in an unlikely friendship when I was a disturbed fourteen-year-old. Without meeting Mark, my life would be very different today.

Mark was in college at the time. He and a few other college students got jobs at my high school in hopes of investing in younger guys who seemed troubled. Well, they spotted me. I was straight-faced from the bitterness of growing up in an emotionally volatile home. And though I tried to cover this up with a quick wit, long hair, and a rebellious attitude, Mark must have known that more was going on inside me.

As our friendship developed, he invited me on hikes and camping trips with his college friends. The deeper we went, I began calling him to ask questions about issues I faced in life. Eventually, when my parents' marriage became too chaotic for me to stay at home, I found a place of safety by sleeping on the floor in his college dorm room.

The summer before my senior year in high school, Mark needed a place to live as he took classes at college. After my parents' divorce, our family had become more stable and to help Mark save money, we took him in, and he slept on a foam mat on the floor in my room. During those months we became like brothers. We stayed up late talking and went on long adventures during the weekends. That short phase of time camping and floating rivers had an impact I'm not sure I can describe—it changed me.

Up to that point, I'd never had a steady, safe, and predictable male-figure in my life. Those summer months formed how I view relationship and leadership. Everyone needs someone who will roll up the metaphorical mat on your floor to spend time together because they care. Mark is one of my heroes, and he's dedicated his life to mentoring young people. Believe it or not, he sometimes calls me now for guidance. What's even better, his daughter attends a university not far from where I live now. From time to time, she comes to my house to ask me for advice. That's how these deep relationships work over the years; they morph into a mutual friendship and mutual blessing. Mark's investment in that troubled teenage boy many years ago has come back to serve him (and his daughter) through *my* changed life. Mark, thank you.

EVERYONE CHANGES

For some, relationships like this may seem foreign. But as you age, everything about you is changing, both brain and body. Going away with a guide will help you get intentional with what's already happening in your physiology. Though the neural pathways in your brain may be set toward certain habits, by trying new practices, you can create new pathways, new thinking, and new ways of being and working. How might that be helpful to you personally and professionally?

Your ability to sustain your work is rooted in the internal and interconnected parts of your life being healthy over a long period of time. People used to believe that brain development didn't change much after late adolescence. Knowing this, it makes sense that such low priority is often given to leader development. If one believed they already had learned what they needed to know, then why take time away? Sure, rest is good, but what else is there to learn?

JUST – KEEP – WORKING.

No, thanks. That recipe isn't sustainable. Besides, now we know that your brain is changing throughout life. This is called neuroplasticity, which "is the ability of the brain to form new connections and pathways and change how its circuits are wired; neurogenesis is the even more amazing ability of the brain to grow new neurons."[39] If you've ever tried a new activity and felt very tired, that's a side-effect of the brain trying something new. It's literally rewiring to meet the demands of the new task. There's a saying: "neurons that wire together, fire together," so what we're experiencing is the feeling of "rewiring." We all have habits literally ingrained in our heads. But it is possible to form new habits and new ways of being if you'll embrace the process. Just try to write all day with your non-dominant hand. You'll be exhausted, I

---

39   https://www.health.harvard.edu/mind-and-mood/train-your-brain

promise. But if you keep with it, it will become easier. Your brain will rewire.

This is why regular time away with a guide is necessary: You are changing, and you need the help of an intentional mentor to make sure you're changing in the right ways. Where am I? How am I? Based on how I'm changing in my age and stage of life, what special work do I need to be aware of? Time away helps clarify these important questions.

Other ways to understand changes in the mind can be seen by simply reflecting on how your thinking has changed as you've gotten older. When we're younger, we have what could be called a "socialized mind." This is when we do what's expected of us. But in mid-life we get something more like a "self-authoring mind." This is when a leader learns to lead from their own inner compass and unique frame of thinking. But the older we get, if we embrace continued learning, we grow to work from a "self-transforming mind." This is when we gain the ability to hold contradictions, get better at finding problems (and solutions), and learn interdependence.[40]

Seeing the arc of a person's development, it makes sense that we need a guide who can facilitate environments for us to continually grow. A mentor probably

---

40   Kegan, Robert and Lahey, Lisa Laskow. *Immunity to Change: How to Overcome it and Unlock the Potential in Yourself and Your Organization*. Boston, Harvard Business Press, 2009. p. 16–17

can't do all this for you, but they are part of the equation. In my work as a coach, I've found that creating retreats around my client's goals and questions in a guided process does wonders for helping them embrace internal changes, and this impacts the organizations they lead for the better.

GET STARTED WITH SELF-COMPASSION

In my experience, busy business leaders are usually reluctant to start a process like this. The demands on your time are high. I get it. But the question I'd like to pose is *how long can you sustain your current pace?* Maybe, for a moment, you could shift your internal thought process away from asking what's good for everyone else, to *what's good for me?*

This type of reflection can feel selfish at first, but it's actually an act of care for yourself. Dr. Kristin Neff is the world's foremost researcher on self-compassion. She asks us to consider what we would say to a dear friend in a time of need. "Self-compassion involves acting the same way towards yourself when you are having a difficult time, fail, or notice something you do."[41] Dr. Neff has said in other places, "unlike self-criticism, which asks if you're good enough, self-compassion asks what's good for you?"

---

41 https://self-compassion.org/the-three-elements-of-self-compassion-2/

You may squirm with squishy sounding concepts like this. But to put it in more practical terms, you've got to treat yourself right if you're going to last. Remember our example from earlier? You're a biochemical engine; are you fueling yourself correctly?

Even as I'm writing this book, I notice that I'm carrying anxiety in my chest. I have hopes and dreams for this project. I have deadlines to meet with clients, and there are plenty of other stressors I'm carrying.

I asked myself the question of *what's good for me*? and realized I needed to reach out to Len (whom I mentioned earlier). Rather than ignore the feelings my body carries, and "power through" the pain, I'm learning to ask what I need to be at my best for the long run. Why don't you take some time right now and ask yourself the same question?

Right now, what would be good for me?

I can't tell you how many leaders I know that can't give their best at work because they haven't done for themselves what they've done for everyone else. They've resisted the changes that come with age or place in life and sometimes have unattended personal issues taking up space. Others are tired because their organization seems stuck, while they are changing. More proactive leaders may not struggle in the above areas but want to clear up the background noise at home so they can lead well in the areas they are paid to lead.

Ask, *What's good for me?*

I encourage you, go away with a guide to get aligned, focused, and have some fun. You'll be glad you did, and those around you will also reap the benefits.

SUMMARY

🔊 Listen

In this chapter, we talked about being clear on your calling and reaching out to a mentor. Even further, when a mentor is unable to give what you need, to create more intentional time away with a coach. Can you articulate your calling? How could a mentor help? We also touched on finding the right mentor by looking at the behaviors of people you admire. How does that shape who you might reach out to?

....

....

....

....

....

⚹ Find a Solution

Remember, as you're aging, your brain is changing. What new way of being, thought pattern, or skill do you need to grasp at this phase of your life and leadership? Based on the type of person you need, what matters most for you and your organization right now?

....

....

....

....

✏️ Meet an Outcome

What results could you see in your life, leadership, or organization if you'd make movement in these focus areas?

....

....

....

....

....

....

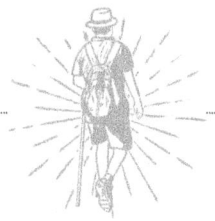

"I really believe that if the political leaders of the world could see their planet from a distance of, let's say 100,000 miles, their outlook would be fundamentally changed. The all-important border would be invisible, that noisy argument suddenly silenced."

—Michael Collins,
Apollo 11 Astronaut

Discipline Three

GO AWAY
WITH
YOUR TEAM

One perk of my kind of work is seeing amazing places. Even better is witnessing the magic that happens when a team goes away together for the first time to a place removed from their normal work environment.

Recently, I was invited to help lead a team retreat with two brothers who co-owned a property development company. Business was booming, but something was off. They knew it was time to refocus to get clarity on the direction of their company. Disturbed at every turn by realtors, subcontractors, and clients, they knew they needed to find a place where absolutely no one could reach them so they could do some deep thinking. We chose a spot with no cell phone service in the best of locations. It was only a forty-minute drive from where they lived: the Hiwassee River.

I've been to a lot of neat spots, but nothing beats the beauty of my own back yard. East Tennessee is home to one of the most bio-diverse parts of the country. We have mountains, rivers, caves, and a host of outdoor activities. The Hiwassee was once the border of the Cherokee Nation in the 1800s and is rich with history. It's immersed in greenery, surrounded by rhododendron, hemlock, and poplar. In the high places, Virginia pine, red and white oaks, and hickory grow. It's also home to the largest and strangest salamander in the country, the Hellbender, which sometimes measures as large as thirty inches. Don't you want to come for a visit?

As we began our retreat sitting by the river, its sound seemed to invite us to sit in the quiet. "Would you be all right if we spend five minutes in the silence before we begin?" I wondered out loud. "That's a great idea," they said.

After a few moments I asked, "As we're beginning this retreat, what do you notice?" One of the brothers answered, "I'm noticing how hungry my soul is to spend more time in places like this. We live so close but rarely come out here." When I inquired further, he said, "Being out here inspires me to think differently about everything, especially our work."

How could something as simple as a change in scenery do this to a person? John Muir, who visited the Hiwassee in the 1860s, had something to say about this. "Into the woods I go," he said, "to lose my mind and find my soul."

After two days on retreat, this company found their soul. I'll tell you more about them and their amazing work in a moment.

Take a moment now and notice your surroundings. Where you spend your time dictates what you think about. That's why it's essential to get out of your regular setting at least a few times a year as a team. Not doing so can get you stuck in tactical mode. Attending daily tasks is part of life, but if it's at the expense of the strategic, you'll feel like a hamster on a wheel. It's good exercise, but you're not actually going anywhere, and you're always looking at the same things.

A NEW VIEW

In this chapter's opening quote, Michael Collins reflected on what it was like to be in space. If world leaders had this opportunity, he believed, their outlook might be different. Borders would become invisible, and the arguments that appeared so big on earth would seem small. Though I've never been to space, I can imagine what it's like to float in zero gravity for the first time. That invisible power that's held me down my whole life would disappear, and I could feel the new sensation of floating. More than that, things would come into proper frame of mind. When you zoom out and get a new perspective, things look different.

In *The Dream of a Ridiculous Man*, Russian Novelist Fyodor Dostoevsky tells the story of a man who has lost all hope and dreams he commits suicide. Upon his death and burial, he's taken by a dark and shadowy figure through the universe to another planet that resembles Earth but is perfect. The man falls in love with its beauty, the innocence of its inhabitants, and its peace. As the people of that other reality become curious about who he is and where he came from, the most horrible thing happens—he corrupts them all.

He witnesses the first lie, and murder, then the first alliance. He sees the first war take place and marvels at the systems set up to try to make peace again. He tries to reason with them that there can be a better way, and they stare at him with blankness and disbelief. "They just barely remembered what they had lost," the man reflected, "and did not even want to believe that they had once been innocent and happy. They even laughed at the possibility of the former happiness and called it a dream."

When he wakes from his dream, he is changed. The vision of another world breathes hope back into him. "I saw and I know that people can be beautiful and happy," he explains. "I will not and cannot believe that evil is the normal condition of people . . . but how can I not believe: I saw the truth."[42]

A change of perspective can do marvelous things. A dream did it for the man in Dostoevsky's story. Time in space did it for Michael Collins. A retreat by the Hiwassee did it for a property development company.

---

42   Dostoevsky, Fyodor, *The Eternal Husband and other Short Stories*. New York, Bantam Books, 1997. pp. 318–319

Your team will also gain a different frame of mind if you get them away from the reality and gravity of their normal workspace.

Executive leadership can be like that hamster wheel I described earlier. It's a wheel of team meetings, strategy sessions, and travel. The corporate world functions from an operating system of efficiency, details, plans, logic, and deadlines. In fact, it's almost robotic. Problem is that robots don't run it. Humans do. And it seems that the types of people who rise to the top have almost robotic like behavior. In fact, one Google study found that a common trait of the best leaders was predictability.[43] But don't jump to conclusions too fast. Google studies everything. And in a moment, I'll share what else they discovered that makes up the qualities of the best teams. But first, let's look at what prevents great teams from developing; the (almost) robotic urgency of the day-to-day.

ROBO-LEADER

The professional world of the 1980s helped create the "work comes first" attitude that still infects our culture today. The 1987 movie *RoboCop* displayed well the thinking of the day. RoboCop is programmed to fight crime. But the bi-product is that he doesn't know what

---

43   https://www.inc.com/walter-chen/google-isn-8217-t-looking-for-stanford-and-mit-grads-it-8217-s-looking-for-this-.html#ixzz38FGlpofX

to do with himself in down time and is often conflicted when memories from his former (pre-robot) life come up. His routine is simple: fight crime, replenish his batteries, and do it again. One day, he's in the police station while the secretary fetches coffee. Unable to engage in the interaction, he says, "Excuse me, I have to go, somewhere there is a crime happening."

The individuals that make up your team probably have a version of that. *"Somewhere" there's a client. "Somewhere" there's an emergency. "Somewhere" I have an assistant who is planning things for me because there's a blank space in my calendar.* One company I work for has an open calendar system. This means anyone can schedule anything in a teammate's calendar if they think it should be there. I know from working with those teams how frustrating it is to have someone else take your time away. Some of us have emails and text messages ding at us all day, even during coaching sessions or retreats. Can you imagine trying to lead a group through a session with all those noises interrupting? In fact, maybe you can.

Research from the University of California, Irvine, revealed that it takes an average of twenty-three minutes to refocus after a distraction. If the interruption was about the task at hand, it wasn't a distraction. But if it did not match the task at hand, that's where problems occurred.[44] It was also discovered that more

---

44   https://www.ics.uci.edu/~gmark/chi08-mark.pdf

interruptions caused people to work faster, but the bi-product was more stress and errors. Working in conditions like this makes it hard to innovate and do the deep thinking work necessary when you're a people leader.[45] If you can relate with this last section, I've got good news. Research shows that creating a great team is easier than you think, at least on paper.

THE BEST TEAMS

Back to Google's study of leadership. What did leaders do that made the best teams? How did they create an environment to overcome constant distractions? Turns out, their focus was on the people vs the work. The *New York Times* article, "What Google Learned from its Quest to Build the Perfect Team," is worth your time. The article featured, in detail, what Google discovered that the most successful teams had.

First, the best teams formed group norms that worked for everyone, and second, they formed psychologically safe environments. Psychological safety is about relationship. It's a "shared belief held by members of a team that the team is safe for interpersonal risk-taking" and "the team will not embarrass, reject or punish someone for speaking up."[46]

---

45   https://www.fastcompany.com/944128/worker-interrupted-cost-task-switching

46   https://www.nytimes.com/2016/02/28/magazine/what-google-learned-from-its-quest-to-build-the-perfect-team.html

Group norms are about the hard agreements we make about behavior. They are "the traditions, behavioral standards and unwritten rules that govern how we function when we gather." These agreements can be written down or not. It doesn't matter. Just as long as there's a shared (and spoken) understanding about how you behave as a team. Psychological safety, in my experience, is a little harder to get. You can make agreements all day long, but how do you get the continued buy-in of teammates to stick to those agreements?

By now you're figuring out where I'm going. The way you get teammates to trust one another and form an environment of emotional safety starts by going away.

WHY GO AWAY WITH YOUR TEAM

The idea of getting your team away from your normal place of work probably isn't new to you. But what you do when you're away might be. After doing this kind of work for over twenty years, here's what I can tell you: forming an environment of psychological safety may be more important now than it has ever been in the history of the corporation.

The workforce is changing—love it or hate it. People are not staying at their jobs as long as they used to. And there's a reason. Millennials (1981–1996) are leading the way at not tolerating inappropriate behavior and[47] are more interested in giving themselves to an important cause than previous generations. Gen Z (those born after 1997) has come into the workforce on the heels of a global pandemic. While the rest of the world may have had years to build relationships, Gen Z has not had that. One study[48] found that "84% of Gen Z experienced burnout [in 2021] compared to 63% of all workers." Why is this? It seems they have difficulty switching work off. "In fact, 40% of Gen Z respondents said they believed burnout was an inevitable part of success."[49] The data shows the world we've created. When everything feels so urgent that we can't turn it off, we've got a problem.

So how exactly do we appeal to the best aspects of our team, thereby getting them to that magical place of cohesion? I'll first tell you how you *don't* do it. Doing silly things and asking goofy questions may "break the ice" but that won't build trust. I was a part of a team meeting recently where the leader opened by asking, "What's your favorite kind of French fry?" That's not going to get you where you need to be—I promise. In fact, I'm quite often on the receiving end of this sarcastic question: "You're not going to make us do a trust fall, are you?"

---

47   https://www.tablegroup.com/enough-about-millennials/

48   See Asana's 2022 Anatomy of Work Index here: https://asana.com/resources/anatomy-of-work?utm_source=blog&utm_medium=web&utm_campaign=AOW2022

49   https://blog.asana.com/2022/05/gen-z-workers/

Trust falls and funny icebreaker questions may work to lighten the mood at a youth group meeting. But they're not going to build a team that will stick together through the good and the bad. So, what's the answer? Let's unpack the term, *social resilience*.

Social resilience is the glue that holds a team together. This concept was introduced by John Cacioppo, professor of psychology at the University of Chicago. Cacioppo is a neuroscientist, and one of the world's leading researchers on loneliness. His work is outlined in detail in Dr. Martin Seligman's book, *Flourish*.

Cacioppo says that social resilience is "the capacity to foster, engage in, and sustain positive social relationships and to endure and recover from stressors and social isolation." How does this capacity get built? First, it starts with deconstructing the worldview that humans are basically selfish. This worldview was deeply engrained in the entire "survival of the fittest" theory put forth by Charles Darwin, who built on this assumption. But could that assumption be wrong? Social resilience helps us think otherwise.

Though humans don't have the benefit of armor, great strength, or flight, like other animals do, we have the ability to band together. "It is our ability to reason, plan, and work together that sets us apart from other animals. Human survival depends on our ability to join together with others in pursuing a goal, not on our individual might," Dr. Cacioppo said. In his work, he helped soldiers understand mirror neurons, which are the parts of our brain that help us recognize emotions in others, learn empathy, and tell the difference between our own suffering and the suffering of others.[50] Thriving marriages, other relationships, and healthy social networks build on the assumption that people depend on each other to survive, to be happy, and to be healthy.

The work of a leader is to give a team experiences that build social resilience. Simply teaching and talking about it won't get you there. But clearing the space to actually do it together—that's worth the time investment.

BUILDING TRUST WHEN YOU'RE AWAY

There are a few simple ways to start building social resilience among your team. Share your interests and see what you have in common. Get the team out of their normal environment to a beautiful spot to foster creativity and openness. Eat meals together. Call on those who wouldn't normally to speak up in meetings and encourage them to offer their thoughts at team meetings.

At the root of social resilience is the need to build trust, which is the confidence that your team members intentions are good and that there's no reason to be

---

50   Seligman, Martin E.P. *Flourish: A Visionary New Understanding of Happiness and Well-being.* New York, Free Press, A division of Simon & Shuster, 2011. pp. 143–146

suspicious of each other. The way there is through vulnerability-based trust, says Patrick Lencioni.[51]

Normally people think of trust as believing someone else will do what they say. That's part of it, but if that's all trust is, then it puts a person on the reactive and waiting around to see if someone will do what they said. When it doesn't happen, they're stuck. So, what do you do?

Vulnerability-based trust is the other side of the coin. It's about stepping in to share when we're confused or don't understand something. Surprisingly, the pathway into this kind of trust is relatively easy. It begins when we understand the stories of those on our team.

When I lead a first-time retreat with a team, I usually begin with an overview of the day with the goals of the meeting. But from there I clear the table and ask the team to share their answers to a few questions I've assigned as pre-work. There are several creative ways to do this, but below, I'll share just one set of pre-work questions:

1. If your life were a movie, what genre would it be? (Comedy, Romance, Horror, etc.)

2. What 2-3 scenes would be featured in the movie trailer from your life and work?

---

51 Lencioni has said this many places, but his book *The Five Dysfunctions of a Team* is a must-read. In it, he focuses his model of a healthy team on the basis of vulnerability-based trust.

These snapshots can illustrate hardships you've overcome, or they may show you at your best (or worst).

3. What have you learned from these stories that makes you unique?

4. Feel free to bring items to illustrate your story: pictures, objects, etc.

At the retreat, before they share, I tell teammates that when someone tells their story, it's kind of like taking off their clothes in front of someone else. To prepare them, I explain how we "reclothe" someone after they've shared: through emphatic responses and question asking. From there, I do a short training on how to do that and start with the leader going first. Since the leader sets the pace for how deep others will go, I spend a little time with the leader preparing them.

The components of story I have them share have to do with their origins (where they're from), their failures and struggles (this is the vulnerable part), what they've learned (their unique wisdom) and how they're still growing (their development areas).[52] Having them share their stories like a movie trailer (as referenced above) is a way to help bypass the fear that many people have speaking in public like this. A great story can be told in about five minutes (with preparation).

---

52 There are many versions of these questions. These are not exhaustive. Get creative.

Since I've prepped the team to be authentic with how they share, they bring pictures or props to tell their story. The exercise almost always takes a bit longer than planned. And usually there are tears. And since I'm the facilitator, I always check in with the leader to see if taking the extra time is all right, since we are usually on tight schedule. I never cease to be surprised when the leader says, "This is more important than you know. Don't stop this; we need it."

I've seen entire teams stop to cry, grasp the hand of a stranger, hug, and even pray after a good session of story sharing. I never plan this; it happens spontaneously. It makes sense, though; a person's story is holy ground.

You wouldn't believe what I've heard. One time a powerful female executive shared about the loss of her husband to a medical procedure gone wrong. "His death is the reason I'm in health care," she shared. "I'm here to hopefully make sure someone else doesn't have to go through what I went through." Then, she opened a box and pulled from it his favorite Eagles T-shirt as she teared up. She let us hold it and smell it, too. Today I remember its feel and its scent.

Another time I heard about a man who escaped from a war zone in another country under the cover of night as a child. In that same meeting, someone else from a different country had the same experience, and when they shared, the rest of the team exclaimed, "We would never have guessed. We've known you for ten years and you never shared any of this." It's normal for teammates who share difficult stories from their past to excuse themselves to regain composure. But almost always, they return to the hug of a teammate or even the simple touch from the one sitting next to them as if to say, "Thanks for sharing; I admire you."

It's brave and risky to do something like this. But as Brené Brown has said, once we go there, we can never go back. Being vulnerable isn't about winning or losing, she writes. "It's having the courage to show up and be seen when we have no control over the outcome. Vulnerability is not weakness; it's our greatest measure of courage." She continues that we can be hurt when we get vulnerable. But the risk of self-protection is that we "lose the ability to connect."[53] Working together as a team can be done without vulnerability. But it will lack soul. Connecting at the level of the heart can turn a smart and capable team into something I can't exactly predict. But what I know for sure is that it'll be better than what you had when you started.

Once everyone has shared and gathered their senses, I share a quote from a book called *The Anatomy of the Soul* by Dr. Curt Thompson. He writes, "When a person tells their story and is truly heard and understood, both

---

53   Brown, Brené, PhD, LMSW. *Rising Strong: The Reckoning. The Rumble. The Revolution*. New York, Spiegel & Grau (Random House), 2015. pp. 4–5

she and the listener undergo actual changes in their brain circuitry. They feel a greater sense of emotional and relational connection, decreased anxiety, and greater awareness of and compassion for others suffering."[54]

"In other words," I explain, "storytelling is actually bonding our brains together. Psychologically, it's how we form attachments. I could have given you this quote up front, but now it makes more sense because you've lived it together."

It's normal to hear a pin drop after an exercise like this because the team has gone to a deeper place. They've truly heard one another—and had the experience of being known and loved. Bonds have been built, trust has been formed, and the foundation of social resilience has been laid.

"Leadership begins the moment you are concerned more about others' flourishing than your own," writes Andy Crouch. "It begins when you start to ask how you might help create and sustain the conditions for others to increase their authority and vulnerability together ... Leaders, you could say, lose interest in self-help books. They are no longer looking primarily to help themselves

---

54   Thomson, Curt, M.D. *Anatomy of the Soul: Surprising Connections Between Neuroscience and Spiritual Practices That Can Transform Your Life and Relationships.* Carrolton, Tyndale, 2010. From the Introduction, p. XIV

but to spend themselves on others."[55] You just can't do this kind of work in your office. If I contrast meetings led in a retreat setting vs. at the office building, they go far deeper when we are offsite.

DOING THE "REAL WORK"

Once a team has spent time engaging in exercises that build trust,[56] they can focus on the real work at hand. Don't get me wrong—building trust is serious work. But the organization has outcomes to meet. Knowing what those outcomes are in advance of the meeting shapes both how I create and facilitate a retreat experience.

There are many ways to get clarity on the outcomes you want (or need) to hit. There's the well-known SWOT analysis, the lesser-known SOAR[57] analysis, or you could take a different approach all together. Personally, I like taking what I call the "astronaut approach" and zooming out on our goals.

Here's how it works. Zoom out five years and ask yourself, where would you like to be? Once you've got that,

---

55 Crouch, Andy, *Strong and Weak. Embracing a Life of Love, Risk & True Flourishing.* Downers Grove, IVP Books, 2016. pp. 111–112

56 There are other ways to build trust as well. Story is essential. But using various personality assessments and creating discussions around how the team works together are always helpful additions.

57 This model was developed by Gina Heinrichs and is outlined in her short book, *The Thin Book of SOAR.* It's a process of discerning Strengths, Opportunities, Aspirations, and Results. It's a more positive approach to analyzing opportunity.

what would you need to accomplish in the next two years? What would be the implications of that for the next twelve months? You could also try the Dostoevsky approach and dream a ridiculous dream together. Ask: *What ideal world could we help create given our unique industry's work? What would we need to do in the next five, or two years to get us there? The next twelve months?*

ROAD TRIP

This is where (what I call) the TRIP towards the real work takes place. TRIP stands for:

1. Top Priority

2. Required Activities

3. Indicators of Success

4. Predictable Follow-up

With the help of a coach, I developed this acronym years ago while trying to discern how to guide a particular team on a retreat. She invited me to think about where I wanted to go like a road trip.

"If you wanted to take a trip from Florida to Tennessee, as an example, what would you need to do?" she asked.

"Well, first you'd need to know where in Tennessee you wanted to go and why," I said.

"All right, from there, then what?" she pressed further.

Thinking for a moment, I paused. "We would need to know how to get ready, and set some timelines for the trip, the stops, and even set the expectations for what we hoped would happen along the way."

"Good," she said. "Now, go and think about how you would describe what you just told me. That's what you're trying to do with this team."

I thought on what she gave me for a few weeks and one day it came to me, while thinking about an actual trip I had to take from Florida to Tennessee.

Top Priority: Get to Tennessee (the "what") to see my extended family for Thanksgiving (the "why")

Required Activities: Set a departure time, pack the kids' stuff, decide stops along the way, and which car to take

Indicators of Success: Overall family happiness and peace which means a stop for ice cream, bathroom breaks, fuel, and keeping to a nine-hour total trip time.

Predictable Follow-up: My wife and I set an agreed-upon time on the Sunday before the journey to make sure we were on track to be ready.

This was simple. I liked it. I think the problem the business world has created is too many complicated words. We get caught up in goals, objectives, vision, purpose, and complicated acronyms that no one can remember (so here's another one!). I hope that TRIP is simple enough and easy to remember. If not, that's all right. The point is, are you clear on what you want to accomplish, why, and how you're going to pull it off? TRIP isn't a set of blanks to fill in. It's more of an internal operating system I use when gaining clarity.

Try using TRIP to plan for your team retreat. When I meet with a leader who wants me to facilitate a team get-away, my first question is, "What would be a big win that would make this time away worth it?" Whatever they tell me is the Top Priority.

Next, I ask, "What ideas do you have for how to accomplish this?" They usually have a few ideas, and I have to go away and do some research to find other ways to help them accomplish their goals. Once we've co-created an agenda we like, those agenda items and exercises are the Required Activities in the meeting.

Finally, I ask the leader how they'll know if we've been successful. What they answer helps me understand the Indicators of Success we're aiming for. These are the outcomes that hitting that Top Priority will get us.

Last, before we ever start the meeting, we put in place a system of Predictable Follow-up after the meeting is completed. This sometimes contains 30-, 60-, and 90-day follow-up meetings. Sometimes it's as simple as setting the next date for a follow-up executive offsite.

THE TRIP IN THE ACTUAL MEETING

Once we've laid the groundwork for the meeting, the time comes to facilitate. I don't always explain this acronym; rather, I operate from it, kind of like an internal guide. Here are three examples of very different goals, and how taking a TRIP helped us meet our outcomes during a team retreat.

An HR Team

Once, I worked with a global technology company. Its growth had outpaced its support systems, and new HR processes were needed. The leader of the HR executive team and I met and decided that the goal was that we needed a plan for how to revamp their HR systems. During our team retreat, we had them share their stories, and the president of the organization came for a few hours to share his, too. Afterward we engaged in some fun team building activities to illustrate the importance of vulnerability and trust on a team. From there, we transitioned into the question of how to address the goal at hand. What they came up with turned out to be our Top Priority: "Remodel HR for the Future."

Next, we brainstormed the main types of things that would have to be done. What they came up with were three items: Create an HR blueprint, get role clarity, and create standard operating procedures. These were our Required Activities.

From there, we talked about how they would know they were successful. We set a number of outcomes we were looking for, with timelines connected to each of these Required Activities. These were their Indicators of Success.

Last, we set times when the team would follow-up with one another, and when we would also sync up together again as a group (including me, the facilitator). These made up the times for our Predictable Follow-up.

A Property Development Company

The property development company from the beginning of this chapter was in an interesting predicament. One brother was the driver behind their workflow (and was the starter), and the other was more detailed (and was the finisher). They were growing and making good money, but they were both tired and knew they needed a better strategic reason for existing. They wanted to create a business philosophy and discuss its implications. Making money was nice, but they were worn out and needed focus.

Since the co-owners were related, building trust was approached differently. They already knew each other's stories, so instead, we opted to talk about when they'd been most proud of their work together and what they appreciated about one another.

During the retreat, we spent time outside the cabin by the river creating a purpose statement for the company and values to operate by. Their purpose statement became: To deepen relationships through making spaces for meaningful time (which is awesome and unusual for a construction company). Finding words to communicate this major point of their business philosophy was our Top Priority. But what were its implications?

Up to that point, the company had focused on remodeling and new construction homes. But they didn't always like the way they were treated by those clients, and they weren't sure they were going to meet their purpose that way. They wanted their purpose to apply to themselves, too, and how they were able to engage in their own families. How could they live this statement out both internally and externally?

They landed on the importance of capturing a corner of the market focused on destination vacation rentals. Now that they had their purpose statement they came up with a more immediate Top Priority for the coming year: capture the "Wow" Corner of the Market. From there, they landed on three Required Activities: find two new properties (that would become destination rentals), sub-contract non-essential trades, and establish a branding team for the company.

Last, we set Indicators of Success for each of the Required Activities and set follow-up meetings.

A Hospital System

Early in 2022, the CEO of a network of hospitals asked if I'd try something new with him. "My team is exhausted," he said. "We've been working around the clock for over two years, and we're weary of watching so many people die from COVID. I need a retreat that's really going to just focus on our own personal health." This was his Top Priority.

"What would help you know that this retreat was a success?" I asked (thinking about his Indicator of Success). "If everyone went home calmer with a simple plan for how to maintain their well-being," he said.

This was interesting because the offsite wasn't focused around creating a team strategy of any kind, which is what I was normally used to. Rather, the focus was on individual health. From there, the Top Priority (for me) became creating a meaningful two days of team building, rejuvenation, and fun to help increase the overall well-being of the team. After some work, the CEO and I landed on an agenda we thought would get us that goal.

In the actual meeting, our agenda included heavier work on story. I asked the team to come prepared to share 2-3 snapshots from their lives that aligned with the vision of the organization: Healing & Wholeness. From there, I shifted us to thinking about our own wholeness. This became our Top Priority for the meeting.

Through a series of quiet meditations, I helped each team member develop awareness of the places where they needed to focus in their personal lives, if they were to remain strong. We came up with individual statements of development, and through interactions in pairs, we created ideas on how to find traction in those areas. Each teammate therefore gained a set of Required Activities that would help their personal well-being.

"What would success look like for you in the next year?" I asked. "This," I said, "is the real outcome you're after." From there, I had each teammate write down their own Indicators of Success and create ways for Predictable Follow-up in their own lives.

WHAT TRIP TO NOT TAKE

I must restate: Please do not read these stories and think that this acronym is simply a series of blanks to fill in. No, remember, this is an operating system. It's a series of questions to be asking as we plan our meetings and facilitate those interactions (for me, often in retreat settings). You may go into a meeting with a certain Top Priority, only to find that the Top Priority shifts a little in the meeting. Learn to roll with it. Your team will own it better if they have a say in what they do.

If you are the team leader and are used to running weekly tactical meetings, consider hiring a facilitator to help you with these strategic offsite meetings. It's good to have strategic meetings like this 2-4 times yearly away from the office. The team will likely open up and participate on a deeper level with a trained coach leading these interactions. Besides, you owe it to yourself to get an outside perspective regularly to help you think bigger than what you see every day. I can't emphasize this enough. Your team is supposed to give you a multi-faceted perspective. Are you doing your due-diligence to set the table to allow them to create the strategy to execute their part in the organization's objectives?

Work together with the facilitator to design a retreat that will achieve your Top Priority. But don't hire an outsider and just assume they'll get it right. No, great meetings work best when they are created together (both with your guidance and their outside expertise).

HAVE SOME FUN

In each example mentioned above, the team leader made time to do something fun during these retreat meetings. I've seen so many creative fun things that it's impossible to list them all. But here are some of my favorites:

- ✔ Do an escape room together.

- ✔ Go play a game or base an evening around a game-like activity like Top Golf.

✔ Once I went zip-lining in the Redwood Forest in Northern California. This one was pretty epic, but there are ropes courses built for this kind of thing near you. Do your homework, you'll find them.

✔ Go out for a nice meal and have some drinks. Talk about your best and worst jobs or what advice your older self would give your younger self. The list of discussion questions over drinks is endless. Keep it light, have some fun. But be intentional.

✔ Take a cooking class and eat the meal together when you're done.

✔ Take an improv-comedy class.

✔ Volunteer at a charitable organization together.

✔ Build a habitat-for-humanity house as a group.

✔ Go on an overseas service trip.

Studies have shown that having fun does a lot for us. It reduces stress, boosts energy, improves your ability to concentrate, and improves connection with others (among other things).[58] Probably the most important bi-product of having fun is your team will *want* to be

---

58   https://heelthatpain.com/8-health-benefits-of-having-fun/

together. We spend most of our lives at work, so that's a feeling I want to have. What about you?

By employing a regular practice of retreating together, your team will be more inclined to move *toward* one another when times get hard, instead of away from each other. And when we stick with one another, our chances of weathering hard times improve drastically. I learned this from the most interesting source, a retired Park Ranger.

LOST? STICK TOGETHER

I met Dwight McCarter shortly after his retirement from the National Park Service. The year was 1998, and he was at the visitor center in Smokey Mountains National Park promoting his book called *Lost! A Ranger's Journal of Search and Rescue.*

Dwight and I spoke about his thirty-year career tracking people lost in the Smokey Mountains. "Someone needs to do a study on the psychological effects of hypothermia while people are lost," he said. "It's fascinating." Later while reading his book, I learned why he said this. When people are lost in the wilderness *together*, they usually move *towards* rescue when it finally comes. But when they become isolated, things get interesting.

McCarter wrote how, in the wilderness, when people were lost together, he could tell the differences between the "alpha" person and the "beta" person based on their stance. The alpha would stand with feet farther apart and would veer from the trail, while the beta would stand with feet closer together and stay closer to the trail.

When they were separated, guess who would be *less* inclined to survive? You probably guessed right: the alpha.

"I find," writes McCarter, "that if a person is lost for over two days, reality becomes distorted. Nearly always, the person located [when alone] will flee from his rescuers . . . the psychology of being lost has taken hold of them. They only know fight or flight reactions. On the other hand, if a lost person has a companion, whether animal or human, they have a tendency to go *toward* their rescuers."[59] (emphasis mine)

The moral of the story is simple. Don't allow your team to be isolated from one another. Doing so could allow the psychology of being lost to take hold. Do you understand now why Google's research about forming environments of psychological safety is so important? By fostering an environment of trust through regular times of going away together, you will help them learn to move *toward* one another, thereby finding solutions that matter most for the team and organization. You'll have more fun, adventure, and rewarding work, too.

---

59   McCarter, Dwight and Schmidt, Ronald. *Lost! A Rangers Journal of Search and Rescue.* Graphicom Press, Yellow Springs, 1998, p.131

In some cases, offsite meetings like this will serve to expose teammates who don't want to shed their biases. As much as I wish what I have written is a magic formula, it isn't going to change some. They have to want it, and you'll have to want it bad enough to let those go who are unable or unwilling to lean in to develop trust. Developing a team like this is hard work, but totally worth the effort.

SUMMARY

🔊 **Listen**

In this chapter, we talked the discipline of going away with your team to elevate their perspective. We also touched on how the best leaders predictably create environments of psychological safety and working norms. What other points stood out to you?

🔍 **Find a Solution**

Based on what stood out to you, what resource might be applicable from this section? The practice of dreaming together? Building social resilience? Getting the team away from their normal workplace? Building trust through storytelling? Or maybe it was helpful to think about planning (or facilitating) a team meeting using the TRIP acronym.[60]

....

....

....

....

....

✎ Meet an Outcome

If you address what's come up for you with the tools you've chosen, what effect do you think that would have?

....

....

....

....

....

---

60   You are welcome to reuse the TRIP acronym. Please cite this book as its origin and source.

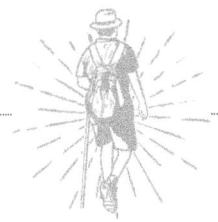

"One who cannot govern his house and family will be much less competent to govern a state, and should not be given power over others."
—Pachacutec (1438–1472), Ruler of the Inca Empire

Discipline Four

GO AWAY
WITH
YOUR FAMILY

When you think of your family, who comes to mind? It could be your spouse or significant other, or maybe your children come to mind. If you're not part of a nuclear family, maybe you consider a close group of friends like family. Take a moment, close your eyes, notice whose faces appear.

As their faces appear, focus on each one. What do they each need? What do they want collectively? What could you receive from them? How could the relationships you just imagined add to your health and happiness if you'd give them the time they deserve?

Now, think about how much time you spend planning for your work. Think about all those 1/1s, weekly meetings or quarterly strategy meetings. Imagine what could happen with your family if you'd give even a small portion of that much intention.

Our last discipline (but certainly not least), *Go Away with Your Family*, is meant to call you to become more intentional with your most important relationships. For most of us, this probably means our significant other and/or children. But the definition can be broader. Consider that as you read.

You may be wondering, *why is going away with my family inserted into a book on being a better business leader?* I'm glad you're asking. But rather than answer, maybe I'll turn it around on you with a few questions for your reflection. Scribble your answers in the blanks provided.

1. How does your family's health matter for you personally right now?

\
\
\
\

2. What family issues are taking up bandwidth in your mind, even while at work?

\
\
\
\

3. What would it look like for you to address those?

4. How could this improve your focus at work?

5. What implications could it have on your team, or organization, if they were to see you getting more intentional with your family?

I hope that after reflecting for a few moments you're able to see that your personal life has implications for your work life.

In this section, though I will make a few applications for how going away with your family matters to your organization, my primary focus is to appeal to you personally. Here's why: at the core of our society is the family. Mother Theresa is attributed to have said that if you want to make an impact in this world, "go home and love your family." To make the point further, Alex Haley said that "the family is a link to our past, bridge to our future." Without healthy families, our society's future just won't be very steady. The business case (I believe) for going away with your family is that your entire organization is made up of family members. The more intention you apply to yours will help them see how they can do it, too. Because we're social creatures, we're influencing others whenever we're together (whether we realize it or not).

LIMBIC RESONANCE

The health (or unhealth) of our most significant relationships impacts those in relational proximity to us. Though you may not be thinking of it, the emotional well-being of your family is rubbing off on you. This sets off a chain reaction that also rubs off on your team and to the rest of your organization. The word "culture" is just code for "relationships." So whether it's something as simple as how your kids are doing, or something as complex as divorce, compartmentalizing emotional energy is hard and barely sustainable. Separating "personal" and "business" impacts our organizational "culture" in tangible ways. The main reason is simple; we're not divided people. We bring our issues with us wherever we go.

I once worked with an influential leader whose company sought coaching for her because she was coming across too rough to her team. They said she needed to "learn political correctness." As I inquired deeper, their HR leader said, "She may need some personal coaching too. I think she's having some problems at home." As I began coaching this leader and our relationship progressed, it came out that her husband had significant problems she couldn't support him in. He'd lost someone significant to him and was spiraling into depression. She didn't feel she could give him the time he deserved. With coaching, she found the permission she needed to work on her marriage. With that, her impact at work softened, and her team breathed a sigh of relief. Her harshness was creating silos. But as she softened, the team began to lean in again.

We are only as strong as our system of relationships. Have you ever been on a team with a colleague whose wife had cancer or whose kids were struggling? Then you know, we bring it all with us to work. Whether we show it or hide it, it's there. And as humans, our brains are synchronizing with those closest to us. This phenomenon is called *limbic resonance.*

Limbic resonance is about sharing deep emotional states with other people. Our brains are literally putting off "vibes" that others pick up on. This is why seeing a movie in a packed theater can feel more powerful than watching it alone. Limbic resonance is the non-verbal communication that takes place between mammals.[61] Why does a snake not react when an eagle eats its young? Yet a bear, or a dog, or even a squirrel will fight to protect its babies? Mammals possess a limbic region in their brains that reptiles do not.[62] We share this resonance with our closest relationships. Our personal health and the health of our family therefore puts off literal vibes that others are sensing. When they inquire and we say, "Nothing's wrong," when we really have an issue, we are indirectly teaching them to not pay attention to their intuition. What implications might that have for how we operate at work?

Focusing on the health of your family is an important part of focusing on the health of your organization because you set standards for the relational patterns of your closest teammates. Take a moment and survey how the relationships of your teammates are with their families. *Where do things seem strong? Where do things lack? What themes do you notice? Do you see some of those themes in your own life?* As the leader, you set the pace for acceptable behavior. But give yourself a break. Just like you are a work in progress, so is your organization. And the work never stops.

---

61   https://en.wikipedia.org/wiki/Limbic_resonance
62   The book, *A General Theory of Love,* by Thomas Lewis, Fari Amini, and Richard Lannon, explains the biological basis for human emotions.

Of all the disciplines in this book, this one is the most challenging for me to write about. I tend to listen to my inner critic. If you're like me, you may be thinking immediately about the things you've not done right. But for a few moments, I invite you to pause and let that thought disappear. Just for a minute, think about the chance that you have exactly what it takes to build a healthy family, and be curious about the changes that could bring for those closest to you at work and in your organization. Let the critic go silent. For a moment, listen to your inner ally.

Years ago, I read Ben and Rosamund Zander's book, *The Art of Possibility*. Ben Zander, the director of the Boston Philharmonic, recounts with amazing optimism how he learned to change the way people think about themselves and what they can contribute to this world. This book helped me restore my relationship with my father through one simple idea: "In the measurement world, we set a goal and strive to achieve it," Zander wrote. "In the universe of possibility, we set the context and let life unfold."[63] (More about my dad in a moment.)

Whether it's your family, or your organization, when things like a recession, pandemic, or natural disaster strike, we are somewhat out of control (which most of us don't get excited about). But even in those cases,

---

63 Zander, Rosamund Stone and Zander, Benjamin. *The Art of Possibility: Transforming Professional and Personal life.* New York, Penguin Books, 2000. pp. 17–24

with TRIP (as in the last chapter), we *can* hit certain outcomes. However, in the cases where we can't control the results, letting life unfold can hold new experiences.

CONTEXT VS. OUTCOMES

In the corporate space, we're conditioned to monitor the organizations health by checking its vital signs. One of those vitals is the amount of money coming in and going out. When things aren't going well, we bring attention to that part of the organization (which is simply a group of people). And even though we've learned to bring this kind of intention to our organizations, sometimes we are inept at bringing that same focus to our families.

What do you think the vital signs of a healthy family are? Remember John (from earlier in this book)? Many of us have our own version of, "In the business world, I pull and push levers and things happen. But in my personal life, it's not working that way." We all have our own life circumstances that seem to work against the families we want. So what vital signs can we check to monitor its health? The main one I'd like to present is this: *showing up*. Or to put it in question form, are you consistently showing up to your most important relationships?

John Quincy Adams was once asked how he was able to stay focused amidst extreme political opposition. His answer: "Duty is ours. Results are God's." If the words "duty" or "God" bother you, think of it this way. In your family, you are responsible to set the table for a certain set of things and you can't always control the outcome. But what can you influence? You can control (usually) how often you show up to those most important relationships. From there, we have to let life unfold.

How much did you show up in your most important relationships this month? Now that's a vital sign you can monitor.

One day when I'm old and gone, I'll be honored if my tombstone had these words imprinted on granite: *THIS MAN CONSISTENTLY SHOWED UP TO ALL LIFE THREW AT HIM.* I want to be like Rocky Balboa, who said over and over that he just wanted to "go the distance." Life will bring many rounds, sometimes with hard blows. The most I can do is keep showing up and do my best.

In my life, my relationship with my dad dealt me some blows and I distanced myself from him in my late teens and early twenties. But something happened that began the healing process. I hadn't spoken to my dad in years and had recently moved to Florida to start my career as a high school teacher at the age of twenty-five. I read Zander's words and they swam around in my head for days. One night while unable to sleep, the words came back. So, I got up at midnight and wrote my dad a long letter about how I wished our relationship could be. I sent it, and a week later he wrote me back saying how much my words meant. That letter was the beginning of us getting a re-start, and I'm grateful. Today he is eighty-eight and we are at peace with each other. Sure, it's still work sometimes, but things are good. How did I do it? I showed up to the starting line with a letter that contained words from my heart. I stopped critiquing the status of the relationship in the past, which freed me to try to create something new in the present.[64] I set the context and left the outcomes to God.

The interesting thing about this story is that, as I've retold it (in more detail), other men have been inspired to repair relationships with their fathers. That's how healthy relationships work; they beget more health. Imagine what could happen in your life and organization if you told your own version of this story? Whether it's a parent, sibling, spouse, or your kids, what's your version? What changes might take place if you'd do your work and tell the story when the time is right?

As a leader and consultant, I'm regularly in front of people telling stories. I'm grateful to have a few tales of health and positivity to share. I've learned that one of my most marketable traits has to do with my health, so I put considerable focus there. It's normal for the most high-powered people to approach me after a session and thank me for my vulnerability. "You've inspired me to act with more intention in my life," they'll tell me.

---

64   Ibid., pp. 25–53. The chapter, *Giving an A*, helped me look past my dad's shortfalls, and appeal to the best parts of who he was in the letter mentioned.

Sure, I'm a work in progress like you, but I'm happy that I've found some small bits of success to share. Hopefully my words will inspire you to create the context you'd like to live in and to see what transformations occur.

HOW I FIRST LEARNED TO GO AWAY WITH MY FAMILY

I only remember a few family trips as a boy (that doesn't mean there weren't more). My family wasn't a peaceful one, so it was normal for us kids to take trips with our mom and leave my dad at home. Add to that, because we didn't have a lot of money, these trips were often paired with staying at relatives' houses in other parts of the country. The result was that I grew up not understanding this strange idea of "family time." I knew other families took vacations and stayed in nice hotels and went to theme parks, but mine didn't operate like that. During the summers, my dad would plant massive gardens, from which we would can food and store it for winter. My memories are imprinted with the heat and sweat of summer while I hauled five-gallon buckets full of green beans through the dirt up and down long garden rows.

Each year at the beginning of school, the teachers would ask the class what they did for vacation. "We went to Six Flags," one student would say. "We went to the beach for a week," another would add. My turn would come, and I was embarrassed to say, "I worked in the garden."

Don't get me wrong, we did family things together like going to the lake or an occasional trip somewhere. But it was rarely harmonious, and the older I got, vacations weren't together. My memory of "family time" was colored more by turmoil than joy. I didn't learn till later in life (in my early 30s) how important it was to form a new, and intentional, family map. Here's how it happened.

One day I was downstairs in our church's kitchen, and I ran into a friend of mine, the CEO of our local hospital. His name was Dave and we'd spent years developing a friendship. Dave's daughters would babysit my kids while my wife and I went on dates. Dave and I would sometimes run together. And even occasionally, we'd meet up for breakfast. I deeply admired Dave, who had risen to such an influential position, as he often told me, by simply *being in the right place at the right time.*"

Our church was known to provide meeting spaces for various events in our city and the result was that there was often (very good) leftover catered food in the industrial sized refrigerator in the basement. Dave and I were both in the basement that day looking for a snack and, as usual, started catching up. Dave is humble, confident, direct, and has an amazing sense of humor. I loved our talks and always looked forward to them. On this day, he was sharing about a family vacation he'd just come back from where he'd taken his family skiing in the mountains of British Columbia.

As he described the things they did, I couldn't help but envy him. He had the financial means to take trips like this, and he did it regularly with his family. I'd become comfortable enough with Dave to joke around with him, and often we took jabs at one another. So on this day, it felt normal to crack a joke. Here are the words that came out of my mouth: "Wow, what would it take for me to tag along on one of *your* vacations?!"

Dave smirked, paused, and then said the words that would change my life. "Well David," he said with a grin, "last time I checked, you weren't in my family."

His words both instructed me and cut me. He was right; though we were close, we weren't *that* close. *I shouldn't have said that,* I thought. Dave's words cut because I longed to have a dad like him, and his words reminded me of my own lack. For years, I'd endeavored to open my life to others, but at that time in life, I did it at the expense of my own family. I was doing in the outside world what I wanted most for my inside world. Dave's words woke me up. There were only a few spots at the table for my wife and kids, and I was crowding them out with my job, with friends, and neighbors. I had to change. From a distance, it seemed David had this one figured out, and I wanted to understand how to do it.

IDEAL VS. REALITY

As I got to know Dave, I discovered his family had issues just like mine. Because that's how relationships are: the closer you get, you start to see each other's flaws. But the real thing I wanted to know wasn't how to get enough money to have a great family vacation. I wanted to know how to consistently show up in the messiness of life to build a strong family. I had no template to follow, so how could I learn how to do it? My education would come in the unlikeliest way—my wife's depression.

One of the biggest mistakes I've made as a husband and dad is believing that the perceived smallness of my life made it somehow less significant. It's taken me years to redefine what "the good life" really is.

Earlier in this book, I mentioned a little about my wife's chronic sickness and migraines. The truth is, Amy fought depression for sixteen years before she started understanding what was going on and sought help. Personally, I just thought she was just fragile and sometimes had a bad attitude. She was often sad, had extreme headaches, and was frequently unwell.

Our daughter was a highly anxious child and didn't sleep through the night until she was five years old. Depression plus no sleep for five years equals a recipe for psychosis (which is losing contact with reality). Often, Amy was exhausted and needed sleep. And the time I'd hoped to spend together on the weekends as a family or after work was often without her. This meant I was left alone with my daughter Ana. Years later, the pattern repeated with my son Isaac. How could I create the epic family I desired with all these problems and loneliness?

I heard author Cheryl Strayed once say, "Don't let your dreams ruin your life . . . We usually don't think of dreams as sources of conflict, but nothing causes more misery, anguish, and self-doubt."[65] These words have helped me make sense of my remarkably unremarkable life. I'm a dreamer, and for me to create a great family, I had to come to the unimpressive conclusion that I had to trash my dreams. My life just didn't look like Dave's, or like any of the other leaders I admired. I had to learn to get off the ladder of comparison and start on my own journey with what was real.

SMALL DEPOSITS

I find peace knowing that one of the things I've done right with my family has been to make consistent space for each of them. When the kids were small and my wife was in bed sick, I learned to be intentional about the things the kids wanted to do. When they were small that meant extended time at the park or bike rides around the neighborhood. For me, this was in the evenings or

---

65 Cheryl Strayed's book, *Wild: From Lost to Found on the Pacific Crest Trail,* tells her story of struggle and redemption. It's also been made into a movie starring Reese Witherspoon.

on the weekends. Sometimes in the early morning hours when my kids were up, to let Amy sleep, I'd get out my guitar and make up songs and invite the kids to help me write them. I recorded many of these (and some of them are pretty good!).

Rather than wish the whole family could do those things together, I learned to enjoy 1/1 time or time with both kids. Don't get me wrong, we did plenty of things together as a family, but my journey towards embracing my real life started during the early years of my wife's depression (though we didn't know that's what it was).

Sometimes we see what others are doing and begin to wonder if we are doing it well enough. Stop it. As leaders, we often work longer hours instead of focusing at home because we find success at work—and that brings a sense of reward. But what would it take for you to embrace your own life and start where you're at? *But my kids won't talk to me and my spouse seems uninterested*, you may think. I want to encourage you: Just show up to the starting line. Don't get caught up in thinking so much about results. Sometimes our desire to see great things happen takes away from the real work of the normal relationships right in front of us.

Today, my daughter is nineteen and our relationship is strong. All those small deposits have paid off and now she brings her friends to hang out at our house. My son is fifteen now and is starting to lean in to ask deeper questions about himself, his life, and purpose. My wife

Amy is a counselor and helps others who struggle like she once did. Contrary to what she thought, the way out of depression wasn't by trying to outrun it. The way out was journeying toward her areas of brokenness and pain. Several years ago, she discovered counseling, yoga, and anti-depression medication. These years of embracing her actual version of life led to a new reality that we couldn't have imagined.

Do you see a theme here? *Embrace your actual life. Embrace your actual family.* Go home and be present with those closest to you and see what happens. This will be great practice for embracing your actual team and your actual organization. Outrunning pain seems like a good idea at first. But a lifetime of running will only wear you out.

My wife couldn't outrun depression anymore, so she turned to face it. She did what the Outward Bound saying encourages: "If you can't get out of it, you've got to get into it." That was the only move she had left, and as a caterpillar in a cocoon turns to mush before it's reborn as a butterfly, she had to weaken (in a sense) before she found transformation. She's now a therapist with a passion for trauma therapy. She teaches me so much and every so often we even collaborate on my work in the corporate world.

Today, we are peaceful and satisfied (most days) about where our lives are at. After over twenty years of marriage, we're finally getting good at vacations, too, but not just once a year. We do smaller trips throughout the year where we unplug and enjoy one another.

Before we take a vacation, we have a talk about each person's expectations in advance. Amy usually wants to sit and knit in the evening (and the morning, and afternoon, too!). Isaac wants to sleep in till lunch. Ana wants to do something fun together like play a game or go out to eat. I want to go see things and walk. So we build our vacations around expectations. Some people go on trips to faraway places to do the coolest things. If you've got the means to do that, and your family is into it, awesome. We've done some of those things, too, but those are just the context for life to happen. My aim isn't to write about how to plan a great family vacation—rather, it's how to have a great family.

From the outside, my life looks pretty good. But the road to get here was marked with a lot of suffering. Yet isn't this also how a healthy team and organization are formed? Bruce Tuckman's model for team development applies to healthy families, too. It starts with *Forming* (when it's new and we build a solid foundation of trust), then *Storming* (where we struggle), to *Norming* (where we establish what works for us) and last, *Performing* (where we get into our own groove). If the norms you've set as a family aren't getting you the outcome you want, then go back to storming. If you can't storm well, maybe you need to find ways to deepen trust (forming) at whatever phase of life you're currently in. One of the best ways to build and maintain trust, at any life stage, is through intentional time together.

INTENTIONAL TIME

I believe that one of the best things my kids can ever see is their parents loving each other well. If you're not married, one of the best things your kids can see is you taking care of yourself and engaging in healthy relationships. We humans have mirror neurons that cause us to mimic the behavior we see. Our kids show us the best *and worst* of ourselves. How are your kids behaving? What could that possibly reveal about you?

For me, my wife and I have been pretty good about taking regular time with each other. Sure, we've had seasons where the weekly (or monthly) date night has fallen by the wayside. But we are careful to talk about it and try to get things back on track. Our dates have morphed from eating out and movies to the simpler things in life like taking a walk around the yard at the end of the evening to catch up, and sometimes meeting for lunch in the middle of the day. In this season of life, the date nights from our earlier years are harder, so we make the time where we can fit it in.

I also try to make a monthly time with each of my kids. My daughter and I often end up at the mall walking around together or at an Italian restaurant. My son likes to shop the shelves at video game stores and is continually on a hunt to find the best chicken in town. Sometimes he doesn't want to go anywhere but simply wants to play video games at home. So, guess what? That's what I do, too. All those small deposits turn into trust built through intentional time.

Building trust with my kids happens by consistently showing up for these times. And while we're together, we talk and share stories about the day or anything else that we want to talk about. I also use these times to apologize if I've done something wrong. And I give my kids space to tell me about what's most important to them. By the way, isn't this how a healthy team is developed?

This is just a window into what my intentional time looks like with those closest to me. These times aren't all serious, though. Sometimes they are just plain fun. My daughter and I listen to loud music; my son and I pig out at restaurants. This joy at home rubs off on those in my work world.

A common saying is that comparison is the thief of joy. I've experienced this front and center. What I've just written is about how I'm *learning* to get free from comparison. I've got my own life and I'm learning to be impressed with my actual version of it, not the fiction-alized narrative I created from watching someone else.

No one mentioned in this book does it better or worse, we all just do it differently. The real win here is if you can say "yes" to the question: *Did I consistently show up for my closest relationships?* If the answer is "no," start small. Start with an apology. Start with a simple walk around the yard. Get humble. Do the work. It'll be worth it.

FAMILY BREAKDOWN IMPACTS YOUR COMPANY

The evidence is there. The personal lives of leaders, their marriages, and families impacts the performance and financial success of the company. Though each situation is different, we know that divorce is expensive (just read how much divorce cost Jeff Bezos and Bill Gates). Studies have also shown that, after a divorce, its normal for CEOs to reposition themselves and sometimes move to another firm.[66] On the other hand, it's been found that often, after divorce, a CEO's personal worth is tied up more in their firm's stock (vs. their own wealth lost in the divorce). This can become a motivator to play it safe in company decisions and avoid risks that might drive share prices down, which could impact personal wealth."[67]

It's fairly common for those who lead companies to give their best energy to performing well at work. But at what cost?

---

66 https://www.linkedin.com/pulse/does-ceos-divorce-affect-firm-performance-tala-alkabra/
67 "'Love or money: The effect of CEO divorce on firm risk and compensation," by Jordan Neyland (George Mason University), *Journal of Corporate Finance*, Feb. 2020, vol. 60

Years ago, the president of a company I was working with encouraged me to read *Executive Warfare* by David F. D'Alessandro. "I want you to understand my world," he said. "Read this."

As I combed its pages, I saw how blunt, rough, and honest D'Alessandro's writing was. He should know, as former CEO of a Fortune 200 company, the life of an executive leader can be downright brutal.

In the closing pages of his book, D'Alessandro says something that, I think, is his crowning pearl of wisdom. "As a top executive," he writes, "you will be lonely in many of the hours you spend at work because you have to make so many decisions on your own. Don't extend that loneliness to your personal life. Not only will it help your career if you have family and outside friends who can offer you advice and support—you will also not be a pathetic and unhappy figure when your career is over . . . To get to the top—and stay there—you need to be able to lead human beings. And the only way to learn how to lead is to live."[68]

How are you doing at living?

---

68   D'Alessandro, David F., *Executive Warfare: 10 Rules of Engagement for Winning Your War for Success.* New York, McGraw Hill, 2008. pp. 257–258

THE PATHWAY BACK TO LIFE

I'll never forget my 38th birthday. In the months previous, during my mental breakdown, I had completely zoned out. Overwhelmed by my life and my inability to work, I lost all capacity to plan. I'd given myself completely on the altar of accomplishment, and it destroyed me. Earlier, I mentioned coming home and Amy had loaded my bags into the car. "We're going camping. Everything's packed," she said.

Riding in the car that day, I stared out the window as we drove down the California coastline. A short time later, we turned inland and eventually arrived in Julian, a small town known for its Gold Rush history and world-famous apple pie.

On the morning of my birthday, I woke up to singing and gifts. I was so tired that I just sat in my camping chair while my kids bought me presents. The morning sun was bright that day and I squinted as I received their affection. Later, Amy said, "Let's go get some pie!"

We wandered aimlessly in Julian while Amy held my hand. We ate, went to parks, and sat on park benches together. Looking back on it, I realize now how that was a timeframe when my view about myself began to change. It wasn't all up to me to care for everyone else. I could be on the receiving end of the care. In my brokenness, my wife nursed me back to life, and my kids filled my heart with their gifts and laughter.

Contrary to what you may be thinking, it's not all on you to create the family and the life you desire. They have a lot to give you if you can learn to receive.

Though I didn't change immediately, I started to get it. The pathway to me being able to sustain my life wasn't in working longer hours. It was in turning, facing my real version of life and receiving what was waiting.

You can walk the same path, too. Go away with your family.

SUMMARY

🔊 **Listen**

This chapter is about embracing your real life vs. an idealized one. Striving for what's better is good. But if discontentment creeps in, it's a recipe for disaster. We also touched on the importance of setting the context and letting life unfold. Small deposits add up to a life of joy that rubs off on those in the organization you serve. The one thing that will kill it all is comparison. What did you notice as significant?

🔑 Find a Solution

What ideas from this chapter could you focus on to help you make incremental growth when it comes to going away with your family?

✏️ Meet an Outcome

If you address what's come up for you with the tools you've chosen, what effect do you think that would have?

Conclusion

BRINGING IT ALL TOGETHER

In this book, I've outlined how four disciplines of retreating can help you be healthy, multiply the best of who you are, and support those you serve throughout your organization. The weight of leadership can be hard, but it doesn't have to decimate you. You can grow, change, get stronger, and become more peaceful, even during times of external uncertainty.

The seasons life brings will sometimes cause your priorities to shift. There may be a leader out there who is strong in each of these four disciplines, but I've never met them. At best, many leaders are strong in two and working on a third. Don't think you've got to be on all the time in each of these areas. Instead, be asking yourself where you need to shift energy based on your needs and season of life.

Listen: Where are you at? What's come up for you?

Find a solution: Which points mentioned in this book seem most applicable?

Meet your outcome: What do you imagine just a little movement in your chosen area could mean?

If you took a 20% strategic portion of your time and focused on yourself, your team, and/or your family, what changes do you think could be possible?

Discipline one, go away alone means . . . to make space for your value as a person, apart from what you can produce. Make time for yourself and get in touch with your inner life. Doing so helps you become a particular kind of person: one who notices. Get clear on your values and spend regular time embodying what's important to you.

Discipline two, go away with a guide means . . . recognizing you are interdependent. You need a mentor, coach, or other helper to help you say aligned with what's important to you and your organization. You're unique and always changing. Your body is sending you signals about where you need to pay attention. Pursue someone to help keep you aligned with your values and go away on a retreat with them once or twice a year.

Discipline three, go away with your team means . . . getting out of your normal setting to predictably take time with your team to build social resilience through trust-building, storytelling, and developing working norms. This time is also about having fun and thinking strategically about what TRIP your team needs to take.

Discipline four, go away with your family means . . . understanding that the health of your family impacts you (i.e., limbic resonance) and the way your team experiences you. It's about learning to accept your authentic version of life. And, hopefully, as you learn to do this, those around you at work will see how to do it too. Imagine how that could impact your organization if leaders learned to engage their closest relationships with peace and intention?

Which of these disciplines are you strong in? Which one needs some attention at this point in your life? As I mentioned earlier, it's rare for a driven leader to be perfect in all these areas. But with practice we each can adjust as needed.

As we finish, I'd like to pick up again the story of Warren (from the introduction).

THE STORY OF WARREN JOHNS

My relationship with Warren Johns has spanned almost twenty years. He is one of the most driven people I know, and his list of accomplishments is impressive.

Warren came from a traditional home with two parents who worked long hours. As the younger of two brothers, Warren was wired to be competitive. His parents had high expectations, and if he did well, praise was heaped upon him. If not, "I felt it with the gaze of disapproval," he said.

Through grade school and high school, Warren held various class offices and was a musician, regularly involved in school concerts. But his ambition showed up in full force in college while he took a full load of classes, was captain of the football team, president of multiple organizations, and volunteered teaching handbells at the local elementary school. As if all this wasn't enough, he also had a passion for photography, which landed him the role of college yearbook editor (a job he had done in high school, too). Warren singlehandedly took most of the photos, and in his drive to do everything to the highest standard, the school counselor noticed.

"I saw the light in the yearbook office was on all night," she said. "Are you all right?" Warren's response was that he'd said "yes" to a lot and wanted to make sure he did a good job. The counselor invited him to her office and pulled out a large piece of butcher paper with colored markers and asked Warren, "Will you write down everything you're doing?"

"I made massive lists with maybe 200+ things that needed to get done, all categorized in color. It was cathartic to get it out of my head, but it was a representation of what I'd gotten myself into," he told me.

When he graduated college, Warren became a teacher and took his driven nature with him as he pushed his students to be at their best. His passion for photography continued and he began getting opportunities on the side to shoot photo books for big name organizations (like the Bellagio in Las Vegas) and eventually celebrity weddings (years later). He did this all while teaching. Oh yes, one more thing—he took leadership of the high school hand bell choir, too, and then things got really wild.

Hand bell choir? you may be thinking. Not just any hand bell choir—this group was the best in the nation and under his leadership ended up playing for two U.S. presidential inaugurations. "It was crazy," he told me. "We had a music tour, albums to make, and at some point, I knew I had to dial back my drive. Things were moving just too fast. Looking back on it," he admitted, "I see that everything was just another step to another step, even with teaching."

"Warren, you're going to burn out if you keep this up," his school superintendent told him one day. "Things were a blur of hyperactivity," Warren said. He needed to slow down and decided to make a career change, taking a job in the marketing department at a hospital across the country. This is where I met him and his wife Kelly.

Warren excelled there, too, got noticed, and eventually landed on the executive team of a hospital in another state. What I'm touching on here was the season of time I mentioned earlier in this book where Kelly's complicated pregnancy put her on bedrest. During that time, Warren's high drive for fixing things became overwhelming as he spun worse-case scenarios in his mind. "My wife and child will die," he told himself, "and I'll be left by myself to raise the rest of the kids. I'll be alone."

Things weren't good when we picked up our coaching sessions. But after some focus, he found a way to put his work down to support Kelly. After months in the hospital, the scheduled day came, six weeks early, and Kelly gave birth to Riley by an emergency c-section (followed by an emergency six-hour surgery).

With the shock of the complicated pregnancy, things changed. Warren started taking a day a month with his wife, just to rest and refocus. From there, he started taking special times away with his kids. "Those were some of the best days," Warren and Kelly reflected. But just when things seemed to even out, a few years later, Warren was promoted again and moved across the country to work with another hospital system. This time taking a role as CEO of a local hospital.

"I have a high sense of the art of 'possible,'" Warren told me. "People have commented on that and it's proba-bly why I've progressed more rapidly than some of my peers in teaching, photography, handbells, or in various health systems. Even today, I wonder how far we can push a hospital, team, or employee experience. With that comes this attitude that I can do more or that we can be better. It's a difficult thing to live with, and I've found that chasing contentment is a heavy burden."

When I shared with Warren about the content of this book, he gave me a valuable perspective, saying, "I think leaders need to constantly be evaluating where they're at and putting practices into place that keep them healthy. I'm not strong in all these areas, but seeing them again makes me pause to evaluate how I need to refocus."

GO AWAY ALONE

"I've not ever been good with going away alone," Warren said. "Maybe for about two or three weeks once I got into journaling and it set me in the right perspective. Returning to this would be good, but right now it's a big hole."

GO AWAY WITH A GUIDE

"I've only ever done this with you," he said (meaning, me, the author). "It came at a critical time in my life when Kelly was on bedrest. Since then, there have been many times in my life when I've been in trouble when it would've been good to have this. And because I didn't have it, I lost perspective." By the way, Warren is currently planning a trip with another organization to get some awareness and healing in some specific areas of his life.

GO AWAY WITH YOUR TEAM

"I've always led high performing teams," Warren told me. "My teams have outperformed others because of the personal interest I've had in each of them. I go to bat for them (at expense to myself sometimes)." Warren shared how he regularly takes times to get his team away and encourages them to embody margin. "I look at my leadership like a dashboard with a series of gauges," he said. "High performing people in the business world are going to be overweighted in one or more areas related to the business because that's what the world values. But I've always been under-weighted on the personal side."

In Warren's story, though the other disciplines have been there, the real area he had a lot to say about was in regard to his family.

GO AWAY WITH YOUR FAMILY

"Since the difficult pregnancy, I've taken a lot of intention to make special time with my family. One of my favorite memories was a few years ago; we took a trip to Iceland where we saw the whole country in five days in a minivan. We drove the countryside looking at snow-capped peaks and lava fields while singing songs from *The Greatest Showman*. But more importantly, we've established one to two trips a year to a cabin my grandfather built in British Columbia. It's something we know will aways be there. It's a gathering spot for us. There's a magnetism to that place—you can only get there by boat, and it has no electricity. We turn our phones off there and spend time together."

When I asked Warren and Kelly about other practices they've implemented, they said, "Trips together are a big thing for us. There was a season where we had two magnetic boards up in our house. One contained photos from a trip we'd just been on. And the other contained pictures of the place we were going next."

Kelly told me, "After being on bedrest, we've gone through really happy seasons of time, yet we often revert to our former selves. But since Riley was born, we often say, 'Hold on, let's go back to what we learned during those moments and remember that perspective,' and that's grounding. We stray away often, but remembering brings us back."

"During the time of Riley's birth," Warren told me, "There were so many people that came to our aid. What we took away as a family is that we want to be defined as a family who loves others generously [in the way we were loved]. Our kids know that we are a family who expects them to engage life to the fullest and to love others well."

Warren shared with me how, in the different organizations he's led, there's a standard vacation package executives get (which not all of them take, and instead opt to receive payouts for those vacations). "Someone on our team had a baby, and after her six-week leave was up, I told her, 'Do you need more time? Work will always be here.' And she ended up taking four months off." If anyone knows how important the birth of a child is, it's Warren. This is a man who wants to give others what he's received.

Warren shared how he encourages his team to take time with their families, and he models this behavior by taking time with his. "No phones, no emails," he says. "We'll manage and the work will be here when you get back." The result is that Warren's teams reciprocate and (mostly) give Warren that kind of treatment, too. Warren tells his teams that when he's gone, to "make the best decisions you can with the information you have. If it's wrong, we'll fix it when I get back."

There's a saying that people don't leave bad jobs; they leave bad bosses. Warren told me, "I have yet to have someone who has left me because of a dissatisfaction with my leadership. Some have left for promotions, but my hope is that they will recreate with their new teams what we've had on ours." It's happened quite a few times where people have left other teams or organizations to come work for Warren. But why? He's not perfect. As his coach (and friend), I can tell you that Warren's drive to improve is slowly creeping its way into his character.

Like all of us, Warren is a work in progress. This is a man who is on his way to embodying the Level Five Leadership that Jim Collins unpacks in his book,

Good to Great. These are leaders who have high professional drive, but also an intense personal humility. For any of us to say we are there would probably mean we aren't. I'm not sure Warren would say he's there. But I think he's well on his way.

FIRE ON THE MOUNTAIN

In late October of 2017, Kelly woke in the middle of the night thinking it seemed awfully windy outside. Going out onto the balcony of their home, she saw a glow off in the distance that seemed to grow and move closer. Within a few moments, she realized a massive wildfire was coming straight toward their home.

Kelly rushed to wake Warren and the kids. While they threw together a few belongings, their small children wondered what was happening. "Grab your stuffed animals; we'll get the pets," Kelly told the kids. Warren grabbed a few important belongings, too, and they all rushed towards their car. They outran a forest fire that night and watched it envelop their neighborhood from the parking lot of a hotel further down in the valley.

Their kids cried thinking about the loss of their house and possessions. "It's just things," Warren and Kelly told them as they watched the fire. "Whatever happens, we've still got each other. And together, we can do anything."

That night, the Johns family believed they'd lost everything, but they had peace. Why?

"Some things you can't get back," Kelly told me. "After Riley's birth, we realized we kept being forced to let go of control and really had to delve into the question, 'How do we make today everything it can be . . . how can we be present with what's happening, no matter the outcome?'"

Being driven is fine, but if it's at the expense of those closest to you, we each need to evaluate what's important in life. "You can get things back," Kelly said. "But it's a lot harder to get people back."

Warren and Kelly's story highlights what it looks like when life throws us surprises and we need to employ new strategies to stay healthy. Taking time to assess one's well-being proactively is ideal. But, as with Warren and Kelly, these moments are sometimes forced upon us. Are your personal priorities in the right place? Is your life aligned with what you say matters most?

"We've gone through a lot of hard things in our lives," Warren and Kelly said. But later the following morning Kelly texted me and added a further clarification.

"One thing we're learning now" she wrote, "is that we need to better embody for our kids how to *love ourselves well*. We've lived so much of our lives in helping others, but how do we learn to put our needs first? That's the area we want to grow in next."

Maybe that's what this book is really about—learning to love yourself.

I hope you'll do it.

I dedicate this book to all the Warrens and Kellys of the world. Thank you for the important work you do. Despite the hard things the world throws at you, you keep getting up and practicing intentionality. And I'm continually amazed. But I hope you'll take time for yourselves and experience the same care you put into the influence of others. You still have important work to do in this world, and it starts with yourself.

"For what it's worth: it's never too late or, in my case, too early to be whoever you want to be. There's no time limit, stop whenever you want. You can change or stay the same, there are no rules to this thing. We can make the best or the worst of it. I hope you make the best of it. And I hope you see things that startle you. I hope you feel things you never felt before. I hope you meet people with a different point of view. I hope you live a life you're proud of. If you find that you're not, I hope you have the courage to start all over again."

—Eric Roth, *The Curious Case of Benjamin Button* (Screenplay)

WHAT'S NEXT?

The Achata Coaching & Leadership Group was founded in 2011. Our Noble Cause is to make space for leaders to find vision. We do this through:

1. Leadership Coaching and Executive Retreats

2. Team and Strategy Development

3. Organizational Health and Leadership Training Programs

We are privileged to partner with people like you. Please find us on Facebook and connect with us via our website: https://achatacoaching.com/connect/

Let us know how this book has benefited you!

ABOUT
DAVID ACHATA

David is an author, coach, trainer, facilitator, and speaker. He brings over twenty years of leadership experience to organizations, team development, and training. He has facilitated and spoken at a wide variety of training events and retreats.

David has worked in various capacities from high school teacher, to pastor, to organizational health consultant. It was in the environment of church leadership that he began to interact with numerous business leaders in the community such as hospital CEOs, presidents of non-profits, and more. This unique experience gives him a window of understanding into the fast-paced world of executive leadership.

As a result of this, Achata Coaching Inc. was founded in 2011 to make space for leaders to find a better vision. Since then, David has had the pleasure of serving top leaders from multibillion-dollar companies and local entrepreneurs seeking ways to enhance their effectiveness, and he has worked in industries such as health care, manufacturing, property development, semiconductors, veterinarian services, lumber, tires, and aerial firefighting among others.

He holds a master's degree in Spiritual Development (M.Div.), and is an ICF Certified Executive Coach (PCC). David is well-versed in using the MBTI®, CPI 260®, the TKI® and TTI Success Insights® DISC colors. He is a Certified Mentor Coach through the College of Executive Coaching and is a Five Behaviors of a Cohesive Team™ Authorized Partner. He lives in the mountains of east Tennessee with his wife and two children where he enjoys trail running, mountain biking, and tinkering with his 1969 Mercury.